D0408055

CLOSING 2.0

HOW TO CLOSE MORE SALES FASTER
by PUTTING THE CUSTOMER FIRST

What the World's Sales Experts Are Saying About *Closing 2.0*

"Cutting straight to the heart of the matter and challenging the assumptions and perceptions that become barriers to closing, this book will help you figure out what's keeping you from closing more AND give you the step-by-step blueprint for doing so. You'll get the mindset, process and technique you need to confidently close any sale."

Deb Calvert, President, People First Productivity Solutions

"In his new book *Closing 2.0* Jeff Shore gets to the heart of selling and closing today's customer. Loaded with value and authentic truths, this book provides a 30-day roadmap for the average salesperson to elevate themselves from pitch artist to customer advocate and trusted partner."

Shane Gibson, Author & Social Selling Speaker

"Finally! Amidst a sea of books offering sales strategy, Jeff nails it with a packed guide to closing the deal. This is must reading if you want to increase your close rate and success."

Matt Heinz, President, Heinz Marketing Inc.

"There is no aspect of sales about which there are more myths—Shore's new book goes a long way towards dispelling those myths."

Richard Ruff, PhD, Co-Author of "Managing Major Sales" & "Getting Partnering Right"

"In *Closing 2.0,* Jeff Shore presents an easy-to-understand and easy-to-implement selling approach that salespeople can use to give themselves a competitive edge."

Lee B. Salz, bestselling author of "Hire Right, Higher Profits"

"Are you ready to flush those tired, worn-out myths about closing sales? Then get your hands on this quick-reading, action-oriented book. In *Closing 2.0,* Jeff Shore shows that the best closers focus on partnerships, not pushiness. If you read this book and take the message to heart, you will radically improve your closing skills and push up your conversion rates."

Jeff Beals, Author of "Self Marketing Power" & "Selling Saturdays"

"In the fast moving world of sales finally a source with fast moving answers to your sales questions. This is the book you'll carry with you for years to come as your 'sales solutions' guide."

Mark Hunter, Author of "High-Profit Selling"

"It is much too cliché anymore to describe a sales book as a 'must-read,' or to trumpet its potential to 'ignite your sales performance.' Such praise would also serve to grossly under-appreciate Jeff Shore's newest book, *"Closing 2.0."* Concise and easy-to-read, *"Closing 2.0"* should completely change the way salespeople view closing a sale."

Kelly Riggs, Sales Strategist & Leadership Coach,
Author of "Quit Whining and Start SELLING!"

"In *Closing 2.0*, Jeff Shore shows how to deliver maximum value to your clients, your company, and yourself. You will get both your mindset and your techniques right ensuring you close more deals faster. Take Jeff's 30-day challenge and start winning more business—now!"

Mike Weinberg, Author of "New Sales. Simplified."
And "Sales Management. Simplified."

JEFF SHORE

CLOSING 2.0

HOW TO CLOSE MORE SALES FASTER
by PUTTING THE CUSTOMER FIRST

ISBN: 978-0-9884915-2-6

Cover design by Peaceful Media and Sixpenny Graphics

Shore Consulting books are available at special quantity discounts to use as premiums and sales promotions or for use in corporate training programs. To contact a representative, please visit the Contact page at www.jeffshore.com or call +1 844-54-SHORE.

CONTENTS

INTRODUCTION xi

PART 1: A NEW PERSPECTIVE   1

DAY ONE: Conflict and Confusion. 3

DAY TWO: A Brief History of Bad Technique 8

DAY THREE: A New Definition of Closing 13

DAY FOUR: The Necessity of Agreements. 18

DAY FIVE: The Agreement Mindset 24

PART 2: THE CUSTOMER'S MINDSET   31

DAY SIX: What Customers Think about Closing 33

DAY SEVEN: Understanding Urgency. 38

DAY EIGHT: The Buying Formula™ 43

DAY NINE: The Elimination Strategy. 49

DAY TEN: The Customer's Emotional Altitude™. 54

PART 3: THE SALESPERSON'S MINDSET   59

DAY ELEVEN: Visualizing the End Goal 61

DAY TWELVE: Bad Assumptions 66

DAY THIRTEEN: Good Assumptions 71

DAY FOURTEEN: Buying Signals vs.
Buying Behaviors. 76

DAY FIFTEEN: Employing Predictive Empathy™......82

DAY SIXTEEN: Dealing with Rejection 87

PART 4: CLOSING 2.0 PROCESS
AND TECHNIQUE   93

DAY SEVENTEEN: The Closing Progression..........95

DAY EIGHTEEN: Why Discovery Drives Closing......99

DAY NINETEEN: Minor Agreements with
Major Payoffs 104

DAY TWENTY: Closing as Problem-Solving 109

DAY TWENTY-ONE: "Almost There" Agreements ...113

DAY TWENTY-TWO: When to Ask for the Sale......118

DAY TWENTY-THREE: The Final Close 123

DAY TWENTY-FOUR: Second Chances.............129

DAY TWENTY-FIVE: The Celebration 135

DAY TWENTY-SIX: Keeping the Sale Closed........140

PART 5: CLOSING 2.0 IN ACTION!   145

DAY TWENTY-SEVEN: The Mastery Accelerator™...147

DAY TWENTY-EIGHT: Practice Tips................153

DAY TWENTY-NINE: Accountability 159

DAY THIRTY: Where to Grow from Here............164

RECOMMENDED READING.....................169

*Dedicated to all the noble and honorable
sales professionals around the world
who hustle every day to be the hero
in their customer's story.*
#BeTheHero

INTRODUCTION

"Business is a game, played for fantastic stakes, and you're in competition with experts. If you want to win, you have to learn to be a master of the game."
—Sidney Sheldon

Gone are the days of salespeople having proprietary information advantages. The world is a different place. The buyer is a different buyer. Old techniques must be retired. New mindsets must be adopted.

Have you ever searched Amazon for books on sales closing techniques? I hope you have some free time to peruse the results of that search; you'll be there a while. It appears *every* expert (and many wannabe experts) has written a book on closing. (No joke: "sales closing" = 10,000+ results.)

So, why *this* book? Do I think nearly 10,000 authors are wrong? No, not exactly.

I wrote this book to fill a modern-day void. Today's best-selling closing books were written years (if not decades) ago: Zig Ziglar's *Secrets of Closing the Sale* was written in 1985. Tom Hopkins' *Sales Closing for Dummies* appeared in 1998. Jeffrey Gitomer's *Sales Bible* was penned in 2003, and Brian Tracy's *The Art of Closing the Sale* in 2006.

I consider these books to be absolute must-reads. (And to be fair, many books about sales closing have been re-released in updated versions.) But I am offering a perspective on closing that originates fully in this new era of incredibly savvy consumers and universally accessible information. Gone are the days of salespeople having proprietary information advantages. The world is a different place. The buyer is a different buyer. Old techniques must be retired. New mindsets must be adopted.

WHY "CLOSING 2.0"?

I believe today's successful salesperson could be branded as "Sales Professional 2.0."

Today's customer is "Buyer 2.0" and we are doing business in "Economy 2.0." The 2.0 indicates a new and better operating system, one that is updated and upgraded. Too many of us are holding onto 1.0 versions of closing. It's time for a cool change, my friends. Welcome to the 2.0 sales world…it's a marvelous place!

A CHAPTER A DAY

This book has 30 chapters. Why? Because this is not a book; it's a journey. I am inviting you on a month-long journey to build new, radically relevant closing habits.

Each chapter is a bite-sized chunk that takes about five minutes to read. Five minutes. Five. That's it!

I invite you to commit 15 minutes per day for one month in order to radically improve your closing skills. That's 5 minutes of reading time and 10 minutes to answer a few brief questions. (Is it worth a whole 15 minutes in your day to profoundly increase your success? …Hopefully you didn't hesitate to answer that with a hearty "YES!")

You will find a daily Big Idea at the end of each chapter. These big ideas are great for "parking and posting." Mentally park on them for a while and, if you're so inclined, feel free to post them on social media. Doing so will help cement the concepts into your brain. Feel free to include a #Closing2.0 on that post! (Inserting @jeffshore would be much appreciated as well!)

WHAT TO EXPECT

This book is part mindset and part technique. In both cases, it is an interactive work. You will find opportunities to challenge and restructure your approach on every page. This is not a book you read; it is a book you DO!

With this active approach in mind, please don't skip over the application questions. You will get far more out of this book when you take the time to journal your thoughts and mark your progress. One of the more important recurring exercises is the Victory Lap. These will equip you to memorialize your progress, a crucial step to any kind of growth.

When you embrace the process offered in this book, your confidence will soar. That is a bold claim. I would not make it had I not experienced it myself and seen countless other salespeople grow and succeed when they incorporated better closing mindsets and techniques into their work. I'll talk more about this later on, but confidence is absolutely critical to both your technique and your success.

I'm excited for you, I really am! Closing well means *everyone* wins—you, your company, and mostly your customer.

Upward and onward, my friends!

CLOSING 2.0

PART 1: A NEW PERSPECTIVE

Conflict and Confusion

"There are worse things in life than death. Have you ever spent an evening with an insurance salesman?"
—Woody Allen

Closing. Such a loaded word.
Is it good or bad?
Is it manipulation or service?
Is it technique or mindset?
What does closing *really mean*?

What pops into your mind when I say "closer"? Is it a title you aspire to? Do you feel like you are *supposed* to aspire to it but deep down, you really don't? Is it a compliment or a criticism? Does it make you think of Alec Baldwin? Don Draper? Used cars? Cologne?

"THAT GUY"

While doing research for his book *To Sell is Human*, Daniel Pink conducted a fascinating word association exercise with non-salespeople. He asked average people on the street to list the first word that came to mind in response to the word "salesperson." The number one response: pushy.

Try this mental exercise. Picture a pushy closer in your mind. What do you see?

- Cheap suit?
- Slicked-back hair?
- Bling? (A fake Rolex, perhaps?)
- Chest hair?
- White shoes?

Let's take it a step further. What do you smell, hear, and feel?

- The scent of Old Spice and stale cigarettes?
- A predictably condescending tone?
- A sweaty handshake?
- Annoyance and disgust?

Unfortunately, the stereotype that springs to mind is all that and more. My guess is that picturing (and cringing at) this iconic salesperson was effortless for you. The predictable, eye-roll-worthy, pushy closer is a deeply rooted image in the mind and expectations of people everywhere.

In contrast, think of a salesperson you know. Not a business associate—picture a friend, family member, or other individual in your life who serves you. Is that person *anything* like the pushy closer we just described? Not even close. And yet, the idea and image of a "typical salesperson" remains in our heads even if we rarely (or never) encounter this type of salesperson in the real world. Clearly, the deck is stacked against salespeople, but fear not—breaking stereotypes is entirely doable!

"Stereotypes lose their power when the world is found to be more complex than the stereotype would suggest. When we learn that individuals do not fit the group stereotype, then it begins to fall apart."
—Ed Koch

THE PERCEPTION SHIFT

It is impossible to continually act in a manner that is inconsistent with your values and your character.

This book is full of techniques and principles about how to close more effectively, but it is all for naught if you simply don't see closing in the proper light. Why? Because it is impossible to continually act in a manner that is inconsistent with your values and your character.

You are doomed if you see yourself as a genuine person but you consider closing to be inherently scammy. If you place a high value on customer care but you perceive closing as manipulative, how will you ever succeed?

This is why we are beginning with a focus on mindset and perception. You need to clarify what closing is and what it means to you. Only then will the techniques that follow have any impact.

"Closing an opportunity shouldn't present any more difficulty to the buyer than deciding where to have dinner. The decision to eat has already been made; it's just a question of the two of you agreeing on where to dine."
—Kelly Riggs, Founder of the Business LockerRoom, Inc.
Author of *Quit Whining and Start SELLING!*

THE BIG IDEA:

When done right, closing is effective, necessary, and an important and positive part of the service you provide your customer.

APPLICATION QUESTIONS:

What misgivings do you have about closing? What makes you uncomfortable with the word or the process?

Do you need to shift your perception about closing? Take a few moments to write down any conflicting feelings you are having right now.

What are you hoping to get out of this journey? What short-term goals can you set right now that will help you identify a long-term vision?

DAILY JOURNAL NOTES

....

....

....

....

....

....

....

....

....

....

....

....

....

....

....

....

....

....

....

....

....

DAY TWO:

A Brief History of Bad Technique

"Your ability to close is not related to the number of tricks you have mastered but the level of trust you have created."
—Dick Ruff, salesmomentum.com

YouTube has thousands of videos on the subject of sales and sales closing. If you watch enough of them, you will see that the same worn-out techniques are being rehashed over and over and over. There is nothing new under the sun, especially so when it comes to sales closing advice on the Internet.

It's easy to make a list of tried and (no longer necessarily) true closing techniques. You know what I'm talking about…

- The Assumptive Close

- The Alternate of Choice Close

- The Ben Franklin Close

- The Either/Or Close

- The Repeat the Question Close

- The Puppy Dog Close

What closing techniques have you been taught that you found to be particularly distasteful?

To be clear, there are times in the sales conversation when some of these techniques could work. The issue is not technique, but *intent*.

In my opinion, the most damaging aspect of so many closes centers around one word: deception. In some way, shape, or form, salespeople must deceive their customers if they want to land a deal using so many of yesterday's closing methods. It can be brutally manipulative or subtly sophisticated, but any technique that makes the customer the victim is abhorrent.

If you want to see the extreme version of sales deception, check out a book called *The Closers*. I'd like to think it is a parody of sales technique, but many salespeople have told me that they have been in training classes where this book was actually used.

Some of the "highlights" from this amusing/horrifying book:

- Under the category of "The Opponent," different types of buyers are addressed by age, ethnicity ("How to close the Oriental buyer"), and occupation. Yes, there are specific closing approaches for selling to bartenders.

- There is an entire part devoted to "Closing by Psychological Manipulation."

- Closers are defined with the adjectives "cunning, crafty, and greedy."

- Part of the definition of the "Intimidation Close" is this memorable line: *"This close is designed to embarrass and shame the customer into buying the product through pressure and emotions."*

- Under the "Think About It Close": *"In most cases the customer will feel like an idiot and go ahead and purchase."* Wow. Just…wow.

- And my favorite close from this book: *"Mr. Customer, I'll bet that when you and your wife first got married you would have bought two of my products for her, wouldn't you? Well, don't you love her one-half as much now?"* I have no words.

It can be brutally manipulative or subtly sophisticated, but any technique that makes the customer the victim is abhorrent.

A BETTER WAY

> With all my heart, and my 30+ years of experience, I believe closing is an act of service, not of slickness.

The Closers purports the exact opposite of what I believe and have found to be true about both people and closing. I believe that as an industry (and as professionals who make up that noble industry) we need to rethink closing: what it is, what it isn't, what it can be.

It is all about intent, my friends. In the unscrupulous examples above, what is the intent of the salesperson? The typical intent is, in fact, closing by any means possible. Which is to say, closing has been presented as the end-all, be-all, "do *anything* to get there" goal.

I vehemently oppose this idea. With all my heart, and my 30+ years of experience, I believe closing is an act of service, not of slickness. My hope is that you will come to see closing as something we do *for and with* our customer, not *to* our customer.

I will go so far as to let you in on my motive mindset while writing this book: My goal was to write a book that *your customer* would be comfortable reading. If this book were about manipulation, no salespeople would dare to share it with their buyers.

THE BIG IDEA:

Closing is about partnership, not pushiness.

APPLICATION QUESTIONS:

What closing techniques have you been taught that you found to be particularly distasteful? What is it about those techniques that bothers you?

How would a change in mindset—from pushiness to partnership—affect both your technique and your willingness to close?

DAILY JOURNAL NOTES

. . . .

. . . .

. . . .

. . . .

. . . .

. . . .

. . . .

. . . .

. . . .

. . . .

. . . .

. . . .

. . . .

. . . .

. . . .

. . . .

. . . .

. . . .

. . . .

DAY THREE:

A New Definition of Closing

"Serve and Sell."
—Early IBM Slogan

I once had a sales manager who liked to say, *"There are two types of people in the world: closers and losers. And if you're not one, you're the other."*

Do you agree? Your answer probably depends on how you define closing. It seems to mean something different to everyone. Perhaps this is why it is so difficult to agree on HOW to do it: We don't really know what IT is!

Some say "closing" refers to the completion of the sales cycle—the point when the process comes to a "close." Others believe the term originated in real estate, referring to the close of the escrow period.

Closing has also been defined as: "asking a question, the answer to which confirms a sale." The late (and very great) home sales guru Dave Stone defined closing this way: "An affirmative response to a closing question can be translated to the closing document." (Dave Stone, *New Home Sales*)

GETTING TO THE MEANING

In my opinion, the real problem is that in practice, the word "closing" means different things in different situations.

For example, is the following a closing question?

> *"Would you like to purchase this car?"*

It most certainly is.
How about this?

> *"Of all the options you've seen so far,
> does this one work best for you?"*

This is also a closing question, but of a different variety. The former is a *final* close; the latter is a *minor* close.

It seems to me that however we define closing, there needs to be a degree of situational flexibility. Capisce?

> "Closing" speaks to behavior while
> "agreement" speaks to outcome.

CHANGING THE LANGUAGE

To simplify the approach, I am going to favor a different word altogether. I will be using the word *agreement* as an alternative to the word *closing*. "Closing" speaks to behavior while "agreement" speaks to outcome. "Closing" can sometimes be perceived as combative or confrontational; "agreement" invokes a sense of partnership.

To fully appreciate what "agreement" represents, let's break it down a bit. Webster's defines agreement as:

1. *Harmony of opinion, action, or character.* This suggests peace and satisfaction, precisely what we want our customers to feel.
2. *An arrangement as to a course of action.* Every agreement always leads to a next step. Always.

But if there is to be an agreement, there must also be agreeing parties, correct? We need to define just who those agreeing parties are.

Our obvious instinct is to assume that the agreement is between customer and salesperson. While that is partially true, the far more important action is when a customer agrees with…herself! Confirming acceptance to the salesperson is nice and all, but the only agreement that really matters is a part of the customer's internal dialogue: "Oh, my word—I love it, it's what I need, and though it's more than I planned to spend, it does the trick. I'm buying this!"

> Our customers are best served when they make a purchase decision through a series of agreements, rather than by our asking one epic power close at the very end of the process.

A QUESTION OF MOTIVES

Closing theory comes down to one question: Who is the close for? If closing is for the salesperson or for the company, we can use all sorts of deception to land a sale. But if closing is for the customer, the most important thing we can do is to make it an easy mental process. The most effective way to do that is to get a customer to agree with herself. When a customer says, *"Yes, as a matter of fact, I do like this model,"* the message she sends to her own brain is by far the most effective closing technique on the planet.

Buying is a process, not a moment. Our customers are best served when they make a purchase decision through a series of agreements, rather than by our asking one epic power close at the very end of the process.

Focus on your motives. Is this for you, or for them?

When it comes to closing, the definition we will use from this point forward is as follows:

> *Closing is the process of gaining agreements*
> *throughout the sales conversation,*
> *culminating in a final agreement to purchase.*

THE BIG IDEA:

Your job is to get the customer to agree…
with herself!

APPLICATION QUESTIONS:

Do you tend to see closing as something you do *for* a customer or *to* a customer? What have you been taught about this in the past?

How does approaching closing by focusing on agreements change your perspective?

Why is it important that a customer agrees with herself throughout the process?

DAILY JOURNAL NOTES

DAY FOUR:

The Necessity of Agreements

"Each mind has its own method."
—Ralph Waldo Emerson

In working with salespeople from different industries around the world, I have spent a great deal of time discussing how we create a sense of mental peace during the customer's decision-making process. Many experts refer to this peace as "cognitive ease." (However, most psychologists label it "processing fluency." It's ironic that they try to make that sound complicated, right?)

Cognitive ease is a critical objective when you consider the way the brain works. The human brain is an amazing energy-saving machine. It is constantly in search of how to make things as simple as possible to understand.

This "processing fluency" approach has a profound impact on the way we make decisions. Every customer carries around his own mental shortcut that sends this message:

Easy = Right

The easier it is to understand something, the "righter" it feels.

Conversely, cognitive strain (the opposite of cognitive ease) feels wrong. This is the mental stress experienced by a customer who holds contradictory beliefs, ideas, or values, and it creates a paralyzing effect. Cognitive strain is what causes customers to lock up.

We have cognitive ease when ordering our favorite pizza. We have cognitive strain when filling out our tax returns. Got it?

While "easy = right" is a hefty oversimplification of a complex brain function, it is nonetheless true and a good starting point for understanding the decision-making realities inside your customer's head.

Your job is to make it easy for a customer to purchase.

At the risk of appearing a little nutty, pause here and repeat that a few times to yourself.

There is a flip side to that statement: *A salesperson who makes it difficult for a customer to purchase is doing him a grave disservice.* Great salespeople make it easy for a customer to purchase. So, to be that great salesperson, we need to understand how a customer makes a purchase decision.

> Selling is about helping your customers
> disconnect from their current situation
> in exchange for a better future.

THE SIGNIFICANCE OF A PURCHASE DECISION

A customer is first created when there is some sort of disturbance in his life. There must be a trigger event (or, more commonly, a long series of small triggers) that inspires action.

For example, why did you buy your last car?

When I ask this question I usually get responses such as:

- My car was totaled

- We had a baby and needed a four-door

- My car was getting old

- Bad gas mileage

Note that the question was, "Why did you buy your last car?" meaning the car you have now. Invariably, people respond with information about what they were moving away *from*, vs. what they were moving *toward*. This is a critical distinction that can help us understand and serve our customers.

Where and when does the seed of a purchase decision take root in your customer's mind? It all starts with a specific event in his life—something significant and uncomfortable enough to inspire action.

Customers crave comfort, as we all do. Doing nothing and extending the status quo might not be the ideal solution, but it is certainly comfortable.

The difficult irony is that the thought of making a purchase decision often makes customers even more uncomfortable than the life disturbance that sent them shopping in the first place! This thought is *so* uncomfortable that they will carry on indefinitely in their uncomfortable status quo unless there is some kind of constructive disruption.

Cue you, the salesperson.

It is not overstating it to say that you are the one who must save your customer from a state of inertia!

Selling is about helping your customers disconnect from their current situation in exchange for a better future.

HOW TO BE RUDE TO A CUSTOMER

Suppose you walk a customer through the entire purchase process. You understand her well and you feel keen empathy and appreciation for her feelings and for the unique situation which brought her to the point of considering a purchase. You give a truly awesome presentation and then…you don't ask a final agreement question.

That's not just bad form; it's rude.

Imagine the pressure on a customer when this happens. Is she supposed to approach you, hat in hand, and ask permission to purchase from you? THAT, my friends, is high pressure sales!

Waiting for the customer to ask for permission to purchase is NOT being a salesperson. It is a blatant disservice to your customer and to your profession.

BEWARE THE RATIONALIZATIONS

In my book, *Be Bold and Win the Sale,* I talked extensively about comfort addictions. These addictions result in a rationalization process I have seen played out over and over. The predictable behaviors of comfort-addicted salespeople are these:

1) They feel overwhelming discomfort in asking for the sale.

2) Accordingly, they do not take action and they do not ask.

3) They tell themselves their behavior is somehow justified.

These rationalizations for why we do not ask for agreements are incredibly damaging, because they actually make us feel good about not doing our jobs.

- "I don't want them to think I'm pushy."

- "I like to just let the sale happen."

- "My customers will let me know when they are ready to buy."

- "Closing is old school; I'm more progressive."

The victim of this kind of thinking and behavior is your customer! Do right by your customers by getting the agreement!

THE BIG IDEA:

Our job is to make it easy for the customer to make a purchase decision.

APPLICATION QUESTIONS:

If our job is to make it easy for a customer to purchase, how is this best accomplished in the process of gaining agreements?

In what ways do you see cognitive strain affect your customers? How can you provide cognitive ease?

What are some of the rationalizations that you have been guilty of when it comes to not asking for the sale?

DAILY JOURNAL NOTES

. . . .

. . . .

. . . .

. . . .

. . . .

. . . .

. . . .

. . . .

. . . .

. . . .

. . . .

. . . .

. . . .

. . . .

. . . .

. . . .

. . . .

. . . .

. . . .

. . . .

DAY FIVE:

The Agreement Mindset

*"There is no more miserable human
being than one in whom nothing
is habitual but indecision."*
—William James

How much does the clarity of a goal affect the steps we take
to get there?

Consider the mountain climber. Every move she makes has
to do with one thing: reaching the top. This goal affects *every*
aspect of her strategy: foot placement, routing, conserving
energy, and all kinds of mini-goals along the way.

So too when the goal is an agreement to purchase. The
agreement mindset affects the entire process, leading both
salesperson and customer on planned steps toward the goal.
The absence of an agreement mindset leaves both parties in a
state of wandering. Everyone is doing something, but no one is
focused on an end goal. Think: sales hamster on a sales wheel
with a customer jumping on for a ride every now and then.

"Forget ABC (Always Be Closing). You can't close something that isn't open. Try ABO instead. Always Be Opening. Open relationships. Open conversations. Open new opportunities. Open up the possibilities. Open yourself to move past a mindset that nothing matters but the close."
—Deb Calvert, author of *DISCOVER QUESTIONS® Get You Connected*

CLOSING AS A STATE OF MIND

Closing is more than a technique; it is a continual state of mind. The effective salesperson can defend every question against an agreement strategy. At any time, she can tell you precisely where she is in the sales process based on the agreements that have been made.

Here is your mantra: *A sale is a continual process that moves from agreement to agreement.*

Learn it. Memorize it. Write it down. Repeat it every day. Tattoo it on the inside of your eyelids so you can see it in your sleep.

> The truly great salesperson builds a bridge, one agreement at a time, between the customer and his goal.

THE CHASM

Consider this image: The customer comes through the door dazed and confused (I'll explain why in the next chapter). His end goal is vague and far off in the distance, and there appears to be a great chasm between him and it.

The truly great salesperson builds a bridge, one agreement at a time, between the customer and his goal. The final agreement is simply the last step into his new world. In this scenario, the customer feels relief and joy vs. stress and pressure. This kind of sale should result in feelings of completion…perhaps even a hug is in order!

Closing is a service. And when it is done right, it is a beautiful thing.

ENCOURAGEMENT

At this point, I want to encourage you to do three things.

1) Develop your agreement mantra. Consider adopting the following ideas as your own. Rewrite them in your own words if that helps.

As a sales professional, I believe:
- *When done right, closing is effective, necessary, and an important and positive part of the service I provide my customer.*

- *Closing is about partnership, not pushiness.*

- *Closing means putting my customer first.*

- *My job is to make it easy for the customer to make a purchase decision.*

2) Journal about your mental journey during these first five chapters. Write with complete honesty about where you are on that journey.

Here are a few questions to help you get started:
- Do I need to change how I define closing?

- Do I need to correct my mental approach on the subject?

- How comfortable or uncomfortable am I with this topic?

- How important is it that I am clear and confident about what closing is?

- How willing am I to try new approaches in order to hone my skills?

3) Last, and most importantly, I want you to rate your closing confidence. Which statement describes you best?

   a) Closing scares me. I'm not good at it, and I am not at all confident.

   b) My closing approach is okay, but I don't enjoy it and I feel awkward when I try.

   c) I can close when I need to, but it is not really natural for me.

   d) I close better than average, but I know I can still improve.

   e) Closing is my strongest attribute; I believe I have maximized my potential.

We will revisit the answers to these questions later in the book.

> ## THE BIG IDEA:
>
> ### A sale is a continual process that moves from agreement to agreement.

VICTORY LAP!

You've made it through Part One of this book. Along the way I hope you have taken the time to answer questions and to really challenge yourself. Books don't make you better; application is what counts!

 Take a moment here to memorialize your progress and recount your victories. Take a victory lap— *YOU'VE EARNED IT! Write down any ahas in your thinking, or any changes in your closing approach.*

DAILY JOURNAL NOTES

CLOSING 2.0

PART 2: THE CUSTOMER'S MINDSET

DAY SIX:

What Customers Think about Closing

"Would you persuade? Speak of interest, not of reasons."
—Benjamin Franklin

Customers prefer a partner over a perceived adversary, peace of mind over stress, and service over manipulation.

Have you ever asked yourself what your *customers* think about closing? The fact is, they think about it less than you might imagine they do. Many buyers would not even be sure what you are referring to, given that "closing" has several definitions, depending on context.

On the other hand, what might they think about the idea of gaining agreement? And what might they think about our definition—that the important thing is that they agree with themselves? Clearly, agreeing with oneself is far more appealing than the old, worn-out idea of being sold to. Customers prefer a partner over a perceived adversary, peace of mind over stress, and service over manipulation.

How customers feel about closing depends largely on their relationship with you. Their perspective has everything to do with their perception of your motives.

A good friend tells this story about her recent car-buying episode:

> *At the very beginning of our car hunt, we visited two dealerships. The salesperson at the first one was strikingly young. (We later found out he had worked there less than a year.) Youth aside, he did more listening than talking at that initial visit and he was completely likeable. At the next dealership we visited, the salesperson who approached us was significantly older and more experienced…and it showed, in the worst of ways. He knew barely anything about us or what we were looking for before he was hard selling us on a model we had already mentioned we couldn't afford. He went on to give us a pitch about a car someone had just returned to the dealership, offering us a "today only" price if we would buy it right then and there. It was clear he couldn't care less about us, but was focused only on moving merchandise. In the end, we bought a car from the young, inexperienced salesperson who actually listened to us!*

Closing always comes down to a question
of motive. How you ask is secondary…
WHY you ask is what really matters.
Are you asking for you, or for them?

APPROPRIATE ASSERTIVENESS

The problem for many salespeople is that they see closing as something negative. In their minds, one must be assertive in order to close and being assertive doesn't seem to be part of the ethical salesperson's DNA. Somehow to be assertive is to be uncaring and harsh.

This thinking needs to change. Assertiveness can be a *great* thing, IF it is in the best interest of the customer.

My son, Kevin, had a difficult time deciding where to go to college. He was torn, and the deadline was fast approaching. One night at the dinner table, I did him a favor. I said, "Kevin, I'm going to press you on this. Tomorrow night when we sit down for dinner, I want you to announce to the family where you are going to college. You have 24 hours to make your choice. Pass the potatoes."

Think about that for a moment. Was that "close" assertive? Aggressive, even? I pressed Kevin for a firm answer and I gave him a firm deadline. I would call that assertive behavior on my part.

But the more important question is this: Was the close appropriate? In this case, yes. And why? *Because it was asked in Kevin's best interest.* By requiring him to make a choice, I freed him up to choose because I knew he absolutely needed to do so and that he would benefit from having made the decision.

Closing always comes down to a question of motive. How you ask is secondary…WHY you ask is what really matters. Are you asking for you, or for them?

The next night when Kevin sat down at the table, I said, "Well? Where are you going to college?"

He looked at me and then announced: "I'm going to Azusa Pacific University."

I said, "Just curious…when did you make that decision?"

"Just this very minute" he replied.

THE BIG IDEA:

**How you ask for the sale is secondary.
WHY you ask is what really matters.**

APPLICATION QUESTIONS:

Do you sometimes find yourself conflicted about the "why" of a close, and whether you are closing for your benefit or for your customer's?

How would a change of mindset also change your approach?

What are some occasions when a more assertive close would be appropriate?

DAILY JOURNAL NOTES

DAY SEVEN:

Understanding Urgency

*"No living thing is held by anything
so strongly as its own needs."*
—Epictetus

You are deep into a presentation. You like the customers and they like you back. You have confirmed the fact that you have what they need. But for some reason, they are just not moving forward.

This problem has to do with what I call The *Closing Triad*™. Three elements must be present in order to expect a purchase decision:

1) Trust Is Secure – the customer believes the salesperson is looking out for her best interests.

2) Needs Are Met – the product must do what the customer needs it to do.

3) Urgency Is Clear – there must be a compelling reason to make a move sooner rather than later.

URGENCY IS CLEAR

It's that last point that can so often trip up an otherwise healthy process. Lack of urgency will kill *any* sale. Because of this, we must have a thorough understanding of what urgency means and why it is so important.

> Circumstantial urgency gets a customer off the fence. Personal urgency explains why she is on the fence in the first place.

TWO KINDS OF URGENCY

Your customer's determination to purchase is dependent on two factors:

- Circumstantial Urgency: what she will miss out on if she does not move forward. This includes product selection, price, preferred timing, incentives, etc.

- Personal Urgency: the reason she is shopping in the first place. This represents the motivating factor that inspired her to start looking.

Circumstantial urgency gets a customer off the fence. Personal urgency explains why she is on the fence in the first place. If we do not understand that reasoning, we can never bring the sale to an effective conclusion. The sooner we understand and engage in the reality of urgencies, the shorter the buying cycle.

Customers who come through the door with circumstantial urgency already in place are called laydowns. That's fun and all, but I wouldn't build a business plan based on laydowns.

On the other hand, all customers have some form of personal urgency. *All* of them. Every major decision is rooted in personal urgency. For example, the urgency to get married is dependent on two things:

1) Dissatisfaction with your current lifestyle (personal urgency)

2) Finding someone you want to marry and not wanting to lose out (circumstantial urgency)

Put another way, there are "from" and "to" components for every type of urgency.

THE ABSENCE OF URGENCY

You've probably noticed that the toughest closing scenarios occur when a customer's urgency is at its lowest. Customers without urgency tend to get hung up on any number of details.

If urgency is extreme, a person MUST make a decision. Perhaps you've been in an accident where your car was totaled. How high was your urgency in regard to getting another car? About as high as it could get. This made your purchasing decision *much* easier, right? When inaction is not an option, the mental strain of decision-making is almost completely alleviated!

To provide a smooth and peaceful close for your customers, start the sales journey by establishing the foundation of personal urgency. What is wrong with their current situation? Why are they here? What is the benefit in buying today? When urgency is well-defined, closing is the natural answer. Get the urgency right and the stage will be set for reaching an agreement.

THE BIG IDEA:

Circumstantial urgency gets a customer off the fence. Personal urgency explains why she is on the fence in the first place.

APPLICATION QUESTIONS:

Of the three elements in The Closing Triad™, which is most powerful to a customer?

Think of times when a close was smooth, easy, and natural. Was there a correlation between the ease of the close and the strong presence of urgency?

What questions can you ask early on that will help you determine a customer's personal urgency?

DAILY JOURNAL NOTES

DAY EIGHT:

The Buying Formula™

*"Business is all about solving people's
problems—at a profit."*
—Paul Marsden

You're walking through a mall and you are feeling a bit peckish. The pleasant aroma of a hot baked pretzel wafts through the air. You notice the pretzel is only $2.99 and because it is baked, not fried, you figure the calorie count is completely reasonable. It's a no-brainer—you make the decision to get that pretzel!

The very next day your 30-year-old water heater gives up the ghost. It was inevitable, of course, and you had already been thinking about a tankless system. While the tankless version is more expensive, you believe you will save a small fortune in energy bills over time. You go for it.

On a subconscious level your brain was hard at work in each of these situations. In both of these scenarios (and countless others) your mind employs the mental shortcut we first discovered in chapter four: Easy = Right.

This shortcut, this heuristic, is a clever and convenient decision-making mechanism that our creative brain utilizes without conscious thought. And it has everything to do with a formula I've been teaching for years.

THE BUYING FORMULA™

People buy when:

Current Dissatisfaction x Future Promise > Cost + Fear

This formula applies to every purchase decision you have ever had to make. If you wrote a sale recently, your customer subconsciously applied this formula. If you have a customer whom you cannot get off the fence, it's because his or her formula is out of whack in some way. Let me break down the formula very briefly…

> Every customer has a backstory that he carries with him into the sales process.

CURRENT DISSATISFACTION (CD)

> *"It's hard to solve a problem when you don't even know it exists."*
> —Fred Heiser

CD represents what is wrong now. Every customer has a backstory that he carries with him into the sales process. This backstory includes his pain, discomfort, dissatisfaction, dilemma, and urgency. It is also the major contributor to his buying motivation.

Note that the most powerful form of urgency is dissatisfaction, whether in one's overall life situation, in his home, his health, or his relationships. Severe dissatisfaction requires urgent action.

We can also note that the higher the CD, the stronger the prospect. People with low CD have little impetus to make a move, while people with raging CD need to make a move NOW.

CD varies, but it often increases throughout the shopping process. Customers with moderate CD might find they have acute CD once they see the options for a better life.

> ### The most powerful form of urgency is dissatisfaction.

FUTURE PROMISE (FP)

Think of promise as a synonym for "hope." It's the promise of a better tomorrow; it is what we envision for our future. As psychologist Daniel Khaneman states, "We think of our future as anticipated memories." Let that idea really sink in. The role of the salesperson is to create clarity about anticipated memories. The clearer the FP, the more cognitive ease our customers will experience.

FP has a way of sparking the positive emotions necessary for a purchase decision. It paints a picture of a better life that can begin *only* when we take action.

Note that the formula includes a multiplication symbol. FP provides an antidote to CD, multiplying the power of the solution. The two are not always initially related, but when they are, the result is incredible power and motivation.

COST + FEAR (C+F)

CD and FP are motivators; they propel a customer to action. Cost and Fear are inhibitors; they hold a customer back.

Cost inhibitors tend to be more tangible: price, payment, hassle, time, etc. Fear inhibitors tend to be more esoteric: making a mistake, change, unfamiliarity, etc.

Too many salespeople make the mistake of attacking the C+F too early. Think of it this way:

If the CD is sky high, and the FP is sky high, how much work do you have to do with the C+F? Not that much, right? But if the CD and FP are both low and the sales conversation quickly turns to a price discussion (a C+F factor), you are doomed. The motivators must be in place before we attempt to deal with the inhibitors. It is imperative to establish the CD and FP first. The formula is sequential!

APPLICATION

This is a very brief overview of a concept that can be discussed for days (and which, in fact, provides the entire foundational basis for all of the sales training programs at Shore Consulting). For now, do yourself a favor and apply the formula to prospects you are currently working with, as well as to those who have recently purchased.

THE BIG IDEA:

People buy when Current Dissatisfaction x Future Promise > Cost + Fear

APPLICATION QUESTIONS:

Does the formula ring true in your own life? Run several recent purchase decisions you have made through the formula.

Think of a prospect who is currently stuck in the sales process. Which of the variables in the formula are out of whack? (Note: It could be all three, but be specific.)

Ask yourself whether the questions you currently use in your sales presentation are strong enough to learn what you really need to know about your customer.

DAILY JOURNAL NOTES

....

....

....

....

....

....

....

....

....

....

....

....

....

....

....

....

....

....

....

DAY NINE:

The Elimination Strategy

*"Customers are human and humans can
view situations in unexpected ways."*
—Marilyn Suttle

At the start of the buying process, a customer can look for
solutions anywhere. She often has no allegiance in regard to
where she will purchase. The most common problem is that
there are simply too many choices. The buyer's strategy we
accept as normal is the good ol' process of elimination.

There is, however, a built-in conflict within the elimination
process.

Two years ago, my wife, Karen, and I were looking to move
but we couldn't find the right home. The market was tight on
supply so we looked for new listings every single day. When
we found a house that looked promising, we would call our
Realtor immediately.

Here's the thing. We *never* went to look at a home thinking, "Man, I sure hope we hate this house. I can't wait to cross
it off the list." Quite the opposite—we always went out hoping to fall in love.

Prospects want to fall in love. This is the norm for buyers. So, what does this mean? Is elimination a buying strategy, or not?

The need to eliminate only arises as a matter of comparison *between viable choices.* In other words, if there are products A, B, and C to choose from, and I could be satisfied with any of the three, how do I make my selection? By eliminating two of the options.

If your product is specifically unique and you can prove that, fear of elimination should not be a problem.

BOUNDED RATIONALITY

The elimination strategy is necessary when considering several buying choices because of what psychologist Herbert Simon once labeled "bounded rationality." The idea is that our ability to make rational decisions is limited (bounded) by three things:

1. Brain power / cognitive aptitude

2. Amount of information at hand

3. Amount of time available to make a decision

A buyer is not conscious of these factors, but all three are hard at work behind the scenes.

The elimination strategy represents the cognitive ease we've been talking about. (And remember: easy = right!)

So yes, elimination is a legitimate strategy. The important factor is *when* that strategy is utilized. For a customer, elimination is a way to reduce the (perhaps overwhelming) number of choices.

> If the value proposition is too similar,
> we are forced to win on price alone.

THE DANGER OF FUTURE ELIMINATION

The task of the salesperson during the sales presentation is to avoid *future* elimination.

We do this by staying out of the commodity trap. We must provide so much value that there is no way for our customer to employ an elimination strategy by means of a simple price comparison. If the value proposition is too similar, we are forced to win on price alone.

A good example of this can be found in the cold remedy aisle of almost any drug store. The customer is faced with seemingly thousands of choices (cognitive strain) including countless varieties of the same brand (more cognitive strain). Adding even more confusion is the fact that pricing is all over the map. So, we end up eliminating entire shelves at a time in order to get some mental relief. In the end, if all other factors are perceived to be of equal benefit, we make the final decision based on price, just to get the process over with.

CLOSING TO AVOID ELIMINATION

Let me share a closing technique that employs the anti-elimination strategy. This is a question you should ask any time you are sensing that your customer believes your value proposition to be stronger than your competitor's.

"If my product and my competitor's product were both free, which would you choose?"

This is a powerful way to encourage your customer to consider value alone, separate from price. If the customer chooses your product, she is saying she perceives greater value.

If there is a higher value perception, it logically follows that the price will be higher. Yet for your customer to then make a decision based upon price, she must be consciously aware that she will be settling for her second choice.

Elimination strategy is real, but it is not the mindset a customer carries at the beginning of the buying process. Your job is to influence the customer with buckets of perceived value, such that future elimination will be very, very difficult.

THE BIG IDEA:

The task of the sales professional is to prevent future elimination.

APPLICATION QUESTIONS:

- Based on this discussion, have you changed your thinking about elimination strategy? If so, how?

- What are you doing, or what should you be doing, to set your product apart in order to make elimination difficult?

- Do you believe you provide a significantly better product and service than your competitors? Are you enthusiastic in how you portray that belief to your prospects?

DAILY JOURNAL NOTES

DAY TEN:

The Customer's Emotional Altitude™

*"If you are not fired with enthusiasm, you
will be fired…with enthusiasm!"*
—Vince Lombardi

I have a friend who recently purchased a designer dog. I can't remember what breed—Yorkipoo, Labradoodle, Puggle—whatever. All I remember is how obnoxious he was in the process. He deliberated for a long time, subjecting his Facebook friends to *all* of the details of his purchase decision. By the time he actually bought the dog, he was beside himself with excitement. By way of social media, I had a front row seat to the phenomenon of a buyer's escalating energy and enthusiasm as he approached a purchase decision.

This is an example of what I call Emotional Altitude™. It is an informal measurement of the attitude and energy of a prospect throughout the purchase process. Emotional altitude will rise and fall throughout the buying discussion, but it is typically highest at the time of decision.

Since this book is primarily about that decision process, it is important to understand the effects of Emotional Altitude™ (EA).

Given that the sales process can be defined as a series of agreements, each agreement is a step closer to the final decision. As the smaller decisions continue, a buyer's emotional altitude should increase. It is the steady escalation of emotion that makes the process fun. (Or, at least it *should* make the process fun. We'll get to that shortly.)

You can create EA leverage with what I call "fall in love" questions. These are temperature closes that can be used throughout the process:

- "Tell me your first impression. Do you love it?"

- "Look at this feature! Is this cool, or what?"

- "How are you feeling right now? Are you liking what you are seeing so far?"

These seemingly small, emotion-based agreements add up to enormous emotional impact.

> Emotional Altitude™ is an informal measurement of the attitude and energy of a prospect throughout the purchase process.

THE SALESPERSON'S EMOTIONAL ALTITUDE™

Protecting and enhancing your customer's EA is a huge part of your job. And let's be clear, it is YOUR job, not the customer's.

The salesperson is the one who sets the emotional pace of the sales conversation. This isn't a choice; it's a fact.

It is impossible for a customer to outpace the emotion of a salesperson. A somber salesperson will drag the customer's energy down, regardless of the customer's initial EA.

This is why a strong trust relationship with your customer is crucial. That bond gives you permission to be expressive and joyful along with your customer. Without trust, your happy responses will be perceived as contrived and forceful vs. genuine and shared.

Want to see a real world example? Visit a Harley Davidson dealership. Harley salespeople are nuts over their brand, their experience, and their Harley Davidson family. They don't invite you to buy a motorcycle; they invite you to join an exclusive club! Their energy and enthusiasm is palpable, and the customers adopt it.

You see the same thing at Apple stores, with Mary Kay consultants, from Zappos customer service reps, and from scores of other companies that understand the importance of emotional pacing.

Let me be clear: I am not suggesting you need to be some sort of hyped up, over-the-top, coming-out-of-your-skin version of Richard Simmons. It's just a simple truth: If you are excited about your product, make sure you let your face know!

> **If you are excited about your product,
> make sure you let your face know!**

THE BIG IDEA:

It is impossible for a customer to outpace the emotion of a salesperson.

APPLICATION QUESTIONS:

Do you hold your customer back from displaying his or her emotions? Can you think of any recent examples?

Think of a time when you were making an emotion-driven purchase (car, home, jewelry, etc.). How did the salesperson's emotional energy affect your process? How *could* he or she have affected the process?

What can you do to enhance Emotional Altitude™ without stepping completely outside your personality?

VICTORY LAP!

As we come to the end of Part Two of this book it is a good idea to reflect on what you have learned and celebrate your progress.

Take some time here to memorialize your progress and recount your victories. Take a victory lap— *YOU'VE EARNED IT!*

DAILY JOURNAL NOTES

CLOSING 2.0

PART 3: THE SALESPERSON'S MINDSET

DAY ELEVEN:

Visualizing the End Goal

"Begin with the end in mind."
—Stephen Covey

Perhaps you have already enjoyed your Grande Extra-Hot Breve Latte for the day. (Starbucks addicts—represent!) But even if you're not into Starbucks, you should read CEO Howard Schultz's book, *Pour Your Heart Into It: How STARBUCKS Built a Company One Cup at a Time.*

The reason I find the book so fascinating is that Starbucks is essentially what Schultz designed it to be. Most companies evolve and transform with the times, but Starbucks remains the execution of the plan that Schultz had in mind when he envisioned the company decades ago.

Clarity of vision is critical to success in any journey. When you see the end goal clearly, the steps to get there become equally clear.

In this case, knowledge is not power. *Vision* is power. And more specifically, clarity of vision.

BEGIN WITH THE END IN MIND

Take a page from Howard Schultz's book: Get clarity on the finished product. Start the race (the sales process) with the finish line in your mind. Visualize the joy of an agreement; enjoy that moment with your customer.

Do you see it? Can you feel it? Good! Hold that thought.

At the beginning of the process, a sale appears like a giant mountain looming in front of you. At the end of the process, you are at the mountaintop, looking back at the steps that got you there. Which perspective sounds easier and more positive both mentally and strategically? Start with the mountaintop perspective and plan your steps in reverse.

> Stop trying to push your customers toward a purchase decision. Lead them, guide them, give them that gentle tug that says, "I am here to lead you where you want to go."

PULLING THE SALE VS. PUSHING THE SALE

When you follow this Covey-esque "begin with the end in mind" strategy, you'll notice a subtle but important modification in your perspective. This paradigm shift can make all the difference in your closing success.

Picture yourself trying to get a large and unwieldy sack of laundry up a hill. If you try to push it, you'll exert tremendous energy just trying to keep it under control. But if you pull it, your energy is preserved and the process is both easier and more effective.

By pulling, you are guiding the process; by pushing you are attempting to corral the process!

When you pull, you are two steps in front of your customer; when you push you are two steps behind.

Stop trying to push your customers toward a purchase decision. Lead them, guide them, give them that gentle tug that says, "I am here to lead you where you want to go."

> *"If you put off everything till you're sure of it, you'll get nothing done."*
> —Norman Vincent Peale

THE CLOSING TRIAD™

In chapter seven, I introduced The Closing Triad™ to explain customer urgency. Your clarity of vision will become clearer still when you thoroughly understand the elements of The Closing Triad™. Let's review the three things your customer needs in order to make a purchase decision:

URGENCY IS CLEAR

1) Trust Is Secure – the customer believes the salesperson is looking out for her best interests.

2) Needs Are Met – the product must do what the customer needs it to do.

3) Urgency Is Clear – there must be a compelling reason to make a move sooner rather than later.

These are the elements to keep in mind as you build your end goal visualization. You should also keep them front of mind during the sales process. Let your focus guide your questions and inform your value sharing as you gently pull your customer along.

Finally, don't rush this. You may need to spend significantly more time building trust with a customer than you do explaining how your product meets his or her needs. It may sound odd, but don't be formulaic about using the formula!

THE BIG IDEA:

Vision is power. Vague goals produce vague results.

APPLICATION QUESTIONS:

How much do you think about your end goal while in the middle of a sales presentation? What can you do to concentrate more on that goal?

Do you find that you are more often pushing the sale or pulling the sale? How can you adjust your approach so that there is more pulling and less pushing?

Take some time today for a mental journey: Visualize the agreement process. Pay attention to the positive emotion, the joy of the decision, the confirmation handshake (or hug!). Get this picture crystal clear in your mind.

DAILY JOURNAL NOTES

DAY TWELVE:

Bad Assumptions

"Even when they are really interested, many clients will wait for you to initiate the close."
—Jeff Beals, author of *Selling Saturdays*
and *Self Marketing Power*

I cannot stress enough how the mindset of the salesperson makes all the difference in the effectiveness of the close. The agreement process is all about purpose and intentionality.

Without this mindset, we are left with a strategy of hope (which is no strategy at all).

It would be wise to challenge your own assumptions and rid yourself of what Zig Ziglar called "stinkin' thinkin'." Following is a list of assumptions that need to go away. But be careful—it's easy to peruse this list quickly, believing you possess none of these detrimental perspectives. Beware the human tendency to overrate our own abilities, attitudes, and mental strengths (psychologists call this "Superiority Bias"). Honest self-assessment feels brutally difficult but it is incredibly powerful. You can do it!

Go through this list and pay attention to any items that resonate with you, even a little bit. That tiny bit of friction could uncover a whole world of change potential!

1) *Assumption: "Closing is manipulative."* Truth: The very word "manipulation" implies intent. You have to *want* to manipulate someone in order to do so. This really has nothing to do with closing. It has everything to do with integrity. Are you closing for you, or are you closing for them? That is the only question that matters.

2) *Assumption: "My customer doesn't want me to ask for the sale."* Truth: This would imply that your customer would prefer to ask permission to purchase. Nothing could be further from the truth. Customers do not want to be manipulated (see point one), and they most certainly do not want to do your job for you. If you want to increase the pressure on your customers, then yes, force them to ask permission to purchase.

3) *Assumption: "I'll know when they're ready. I can see the buying signals."* Truth: Buying signals are overrated. I'll talk more about this in chapter 14, but know that relying on buying signals will get you into all kinds of trouble. Looking for buying signals is like looking into a crystal ball to see into the mind and intentions of your customer. Good luck with that.

4) *Assumption: "The only close that really matters is the final close."* Truth: This is where so many salespeople get in trouble. I'll address this more in part four, but putting all your hope on the final close is a sure-fire way of blindsiding your customer. Pay attention when we get to the part about establishing a "decision-making rhythm."

5) *Assumption: "I'm not a pushy salesperson. I like to let the sale happen."* Truth: Don't be pushy, be pull-y! (See chapter 11). Not being pushy does not mean simply "letting the

sale happen." When you take this approach, the process will invariably derail. YOU are the salesperson. YOU are the professional. YOU lead the process.

6) *Assumption: "I don't want to ruin the trust relationship I have built."* Truth: Face it—if you can destroy the entire trust relationship by asking for the sale, there wasn't much of a relationship to start with. If your customers know you have their best interests in mind, there is little risk of destroying your relationship.

7) *Assumption: "Closing is old school."* Truth: Manipulation is old school. Deception is old school. Intimidation is old school. When performed properly, closing for agreements is fresh and very much welcomed by your customer.

8) *Assumption: "I'm more of a soft-sell type of salesperson."* Truth: We *have* to get it out of our minds that the very thought of closing is synonymous with "hard sell." You want to be soft sell? Fine. Call it what you will. It still does not absolve you of doing your job.

THE BIG IDEA:

**"Whether you think you can
or you think you can't, you're right."
—Henry Ford**

APPLICATION QUESTIONS:

Did any of the eight assumptions ring true for you? If not, re-read the list and ask if you are being honest with yourself.

What can you do to eliminate the negative assumption(s) you have identified? What is a healthy mindset you can adopt instead?

Consider bringing this list to a sales meeting or discussing the topic with your peers. Some of these negative assumptions may be present inside the minds of your colleagues as well. Brainstorm together how to rid yourselves of this "stinkin' thinkin'" once and for all!

DAILY JOURNAL NOTES

DAY THIRTEEN:

Good Assumptions

*"The happiness in your life depends
upon the quality of your thoughts."*
—Marcus Aurelius

Closing in your customer's best interest
is the courteous and polite thing to do.

Having laid waste to the negative assumptions, let's move on to the positive. Once again, think of this as a checklist. Go through it carefully, take notes, and pause on each entry.

Ask yourself, "How much do I believe this?" Then, identify the beliefs that will make the biggest impact on your future success.

1. *Closing is Completion.* It's not just the completion of the sales process. More importantly, it is the completion of the customer's mission. Stop thinking this is about you—it's not! A buyer-centric approach will force you to understand that the benefit of closing questions goes to your customer.

2. *Closing is Polite.* In the inverse, *not* closing is impolite. Forcing a customer to come to you, hat-in-hand, asking

for permission to buy your product is just rude. Closing in your customer's best interest is the courteous and polite thing to do.

3. *Closing is Expected.* Take a look at your business card. Is there anything on it that suggests you are a salesperson? Think of your customers' perspective. Do they not understand that this is a sales process? Of course they do. Do you really believe your closing question is going to shock them? Salesperson: *"Would you like to purchase this?"* Customer: *"Oh…Oh…Is that what we were doing here? I had no idea."* It's silly. Everyone knows what is happening. Roll with it, my friends.

4. *Closing is Art.* Performance art, to be specific. I might be able to play "Georgia On My Mind" well enough for you to recognize it, but you would not describe my piano stylings as "art." There are subtle and important nuances that transform a song into an art form. This reminds me of the witticism from years past: Question: *"Excuse me, can you tell me how to get to Carnegie Hall?"* Answer: *"Practice, practice, practice."* Like any art form, closing takes a lot of hard work and perseverance to make it beautiful.

5. *Closing is Relational.* I am floored by books that claim to be customer-service friendly, but then espouse deception and manipulation when it comes to the close. The close is an extension of the service you provide to your customer. As such, the close should be as relational as any other part of the process. Here's a tip: Think of how you would close your sister or your best friend. Do that with *all* your customers.

6. *Closing is Joyous.* The close is the fulfillment of the customer's mission. As such, this should be a happy time. Too often, the salesperson doesn't allow for the release of emotion. (Go back and re-read Chapter 10 if this is you.) If the close is not a happy time for your customer, you're doing it wrong.

7. *Closing is Providing.* If you want to get good at the close, it pays to think about what happens next. After the transaction is complete, your customer is living in a different world. Hers is a new and better reality. Her life has improved. She is more satisfied and fulfilled. And all because you did your job!

8. *Closing is Assertive.* Be careful about definitions. There is a world of difference between being assertive and being forceful. Once again, what matters is intent. If your intention is to truly serve your customer, there are times when being assertive is absolutely the right thing to do. *"I hope you will trust me when I say that I would not lead you in the wrong direction. If I didn't think this was right for you, I would absolutely say so. Trust me, this is the right thing to do."* How a customer accepts that phrase depends entirely on the level of trust that has been established.

Think of how you would close your sister
or your best friend.
Do that with *all* your customers.

---

*"It has been my philosophy of life that
difficulties vanish when faced boldly."*
—Isaac Asimov

THE BIG IDEA:

Your beliefs about closing drive your actions and behaviors about closing.

APPLICATION QUESTIONS:

Did any of the statements above cause you discomfort? What is that discomfort telling you?

What one assumption from this chapter's lesson would make the biggest difference to your success if you were to internalize it and change your beliefs?

Who can you talk with about these assumptions? How soon can you do that?

DAILY JOURNAL NOTES

DAY FOURTEEN:

Buying Signals vs. Buying Behaviors

"People love to talk but hate to listen. Listening is not merely not talking, though even that is beyond most of our powers; it means taking a vigorous, human interest in what is being told us. You can listen like a blank wall or like a splendid auditorium where every sound comes back fuller and richer."
—Alice Duer Miller

A Google search of the term "Buying Signals" yields tens of thousands of entries. Clearly, there is no shortage of opinion on the subject. Here's the problem: Most of what you read in these entries is fairly shallow and often based only loosely on true psychological research.

Take, for example, this advice in an article from the website changingminds.org: *"If they touch their wallet or purse and especially if they get out cash or credit card, this is a very strong signal for you."* Wow, thanks so much for that tip. Profound insight right there. I would have never guessed.

Jeffrey Gitomer suggests the following about buying signals in his (most excellent) book *The Sales Bible*:

"Question: When is the prospect ready to buy?
Answer: He'll tell you if you just pay attention."

Gitomer's premise suggests that buying signals always exist and that it is only a matter of the salesperson paying attention and responding properly. I can agree with that in part, but I also believe we need to expand on it based on this premise: Watching for buying signals is a very passive approach.

But what if we take this concept one step further? What if we recast the discussion away from watching for "buying signals" and, instead, strategically and tactically design the sales presentation to bring out "buying behaviors"?

Looking for "buying signals" brings to mind a passive activity. Bringing out buying behaviors is all about actively advancing the sale.

Buying Signals (Passive)	Buying Behaviors (Active)
Reactive	Proactive
Wait, watch and hope	Strategic and tactical
Tied to the buyer's physical cues	Tied to the buyer's emotional mission
Puts the burden on the buyer to advance the sale	Salesperson takes a leadership role to advance the sale

Allow me to offer three quick thoughts on how a fresh focus on "buying behaviors" can help you close the sale:

1) *The most important buying behavior is a conversation.*

One of the problems with the study of "buying signals" is that salespeople mistakenly look for said signals as proof that a prospect is legitimate. In the absence of "buying signals," they discount the value of a prospect. This is a huge mistake!

Basing buyer legitimacy on "buying signals" puts an unreasonable amount of pressure on the customer to perform for you. Stop thinking there has to be some magic moment, some specific body language, some killer question.

Here is a human being talking with you, a salesperson, about buying your product. That sounds like a buying behavior to me!

2) *Buying behaviors are about attitude—your attitude.*

The late Dr. Wayne Dyer once said, *"When you change the way you look at things, the things you look at change."* Truth. Now what if we substituted the word "buyers"? ... *"When you change the way you look at buyers, the buyers you look at change."*

Your attitude inspires buying behaviors. When you truly believe that you can—and will—solve your customer's mission, you will actually begin to engage with her on an emotional level. And once you begin engaging on an emotional level, that's when you open the pathway for buying behaviors to emerge.

By the way, there is no downside to being "all in" as a salesperson. But there is a lot of downside to relying on "buying signals." What if you improperly interpret a "buying signal"? Or what if you blow off a buyer because you don't think you see "buying signals"?

Instead, start assuming the sale! Be all in! Be committed to the customer and stay focused on building up her emotional buying behaviors. You'll find out really fast that it's quite contagious!

3) *Your job is to bring out the buying behaviors.*

This is really what gaining agreements is all about. The entire closing process is designed to bring about a very specific buying behavior. That behavior is what we know as the word "Yes."

Is there a more powerful buying behavior out there than an agreement?

It is time to stop passively looking for buying signals and start actively drawing out buying behaviors. Get your agreement questions right, get to work on meeting your customer's needs on an emotional level and the buying behaviors will become obvious.

> *Your* attitude inspires
> buying behaviors.

A SHORT LIST OF BUYING BEHAVIORS

- Sharing what got them looking in the first place

- Opening up about their current pain points

- Describing a future promise where their problem is solved

- Agreeing that you understand their current problem

- Agreeing that you understand their future promise

- Agreeing that your product solves their problem

- Agreeing that your product fulfills their future promise

- Expressing doubt about the decision

- Working through solutions to their doubt

- Agreeing that they would like to move forward

THE BIG IDEA:

Stop waiting for buying signals.
Instead, bring out buying behaviors.

APPLICATION QUESTIONS:

Do you think too much about watching for buying signals? If so, do you need to change the way you see your role?

How can you improve your ability to see the best in a prospect without waiting for a specific buying signal? What can you do to inspire buyer behaviors?

What is the most important takeaway from this conversation? What can you put into action today?

DAILY JOURNAL NOTES

DAY FIFTEEN:

Employing Predictive Empathy™

"Strive not to be a success, but rather to be of value."
—Albert Einstein

When my mother passed away two years ago, I came to fully appreciate the role of hospice workers. These people are cut out of some other cloth than that of mere mortals. Their ability to empathize with people going through an intensely difficult time is extraordinary.

But there is even more to it than that.

I highly recommend you take a few minutes to watch an outstanding video by the author, speaker, and scholar, Brené Brown. Go to YouTube.com and type "Brene Brown on Empathy, RSA." This is a masterful (and fun) explanation on the place for empathy in relationships.

Sympathy is about feeling *for* someone. Empathy is about feeling *with* someone.

Sympathy is passive. Empathy is active.

Empathy is better than sympathy.

Better still is Predictive Empathy™.

If empathy is feeling what another person feels, Predictive Empathy™ is feeling what another person feels *before* he feels it.

Our hospice worker was able to help so profoundly because she anticipated our emotions before we actually felt them. She prepared us for what we were about to go through. She took specific steps in anticipation of our experience, and it made all the difference in the world.

> Predictive Empathy™ is feeling what another person feels *before* he feels it.

PREDICTIVE EMPATHY™ IN THE SALES PROCESS

Who knows more about the purchase process—you or your customers? While your customers may know more about themselves, you are the one who knows the purchase process better. You know what they will go through even before they go through it.

The power of Predictive Empathy™ comes with anticipating emotional altitude and responding *in advance* of pivotal moments. When I bought my first Infiniti (I'm on my fourth), there was a "key ceremony." The dealership knew that getting the keys to a new car is an emotionally powerful time, so they played it up with a little ceremony. It was magical, and I've never forgotten it.

A mortgage lender I know regularly states the following during appointments with new customers: "This is all going to seem scary, but I am going to be with you to make it as easy as possible. My job is to anticipate problems and solve them before they get to you."

Imagine if you were a first-time homebuyer and you heard that from your lender.

PREDICTIVE EMPATHY™ IN ACTION

Let me make this suggestion: Think of a customer you are currently working with. Go through a mental checklist of her life and her situation. Now ask yourself, "What will she soon be feeling, and how can I help her in advance of that moment?" This exercise is best done with your peers so you can bounce ideas off each other.

The power of Predictive Empathy™ lies in a relational connection buyers rarely experience.

And trust me, it is a gift to your customer.

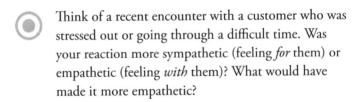

THE BIG IDEA:

The truly great salesperson solves problems the customer doesn't even know she has.

APPLICATION QUESTIONS:

Think of a recent encounter with a customer who was stressed out or going through a difficult time. Was your reaction more sympathetic (feeling *for* them) or empathetic (feeling *with* them)? What would have made it more empathetic?

Think of a time when you were the recipient of Predictive Empathy™. How did you feel?

Go through your sales process and look for those moments when emotional altitude is likely to be high. Then ask the question, "What can I do to enhance this moment? What steps can I take *before* the customer goes through this experience?" This will take some time, but it is well worth it.

DAILY JOURNAL NOTES

. . . .

. . . .

. . . .

. . . .

. . . .

. . . .

. . . .

. . . .

. . . .

. . . .

. . . .

. . . .

. . . .

. . . .

. . . .

. . . .

. . . .

. . . .

DAY SIXTEEN:

Dealing with Rejection

*"I take rejection as someone blowing
a bugle in my ear to wake me up and
get going, rather than retreat."*
—Sylvester Stallone

I'll be honest—I don't like rejection. I'm competitive. I don't like to lose. Rejection feels like losing. The old school training suggests we should be happy when we are rejected. After all, "Every 'no' brings me one step closer to a 'yes.' " Yeah, whatever.

THE NEUROSCIENCE OF REJECTION

The fact of the matter is that rejection hurts. No, really. It literally hurts. MRI studies show that the same areas of our brain are activated when we feel rejected as when we feel physical pain. Our brains process bodily pain and nonphysical rejection in similar ways. Little-known fact: Tylenol can help you feel better when you are emotionally down, even if you aren't experiencing any physical pain (though in my own experience, carrot cake always works!).

Rejection in sales is an obvious reality. There is simply no way around it, and I'm not going to throw a bunch of hackneyed lines at you to try and disguise that fact. What *will* help is to gain a greater understanding of what rejection is. Let's frame this discussion with a very important question: *Rejection of what?*

A buyer rejects a concept, not a person.

REJECTION OF WHAT?

Too often, we interpret rejection through a personal lens. We think rejection is all about us, as if we have done something wrong. In actuality, this kind of perspective is inherently self-centered and egotistical. That sounds harsh and perhaps even offensive, but bear with me. If you feel personally rejected as a salesperson, it is because you are mistakenly thinking the process is about you. It is not.

A buyer rejects a concept, not a person. He rejects the agreement, not the sales professional. When a customer rejects a salesperson's invitation to purchase, it simply means that the buying formula is out of whack. The scale is still tipped in the negative direction and *that* is why rejection happens.

If I can accept that rejection is about the purchase concept and not about me as a salesperson, I stay out of pain mode and I move into action mode. I can focus on figuring out what exactly is out of whack…what needs to change? How can I help?

Please, PLEASE stop confusing concept rejection with personal rejection. You'll be doing everyone involved a big favor.

*"People fear change because it
undermines their security."*
—Thomas R. Bennett III

WHAT THE "OLD SCHOOL" GOT RIGHT

Rejection is gonna happen. If it's not happening, you're not doing your job. Too many salespeople delay and neglect the closing question for fear of a possible rejection by the customer.

This is an irrational fear! If the relationship is where it needs to be and you feel in your gut that the value is there, you MUST ask, even if the answer is "no." A "no" leads to further discovery, allowing you to figure out what isn't lining up.

*"If you aren't asking your prospective client
for their business, then you are not selling."*
—Anthony Iannarino, TheSalesBlog.com

THE BIG IDEA:
Failure is not rejection. Failure is not asking.

APPLICATION QUESTIONS:

Do you sometimes confuse personal rejection with concept rejection? How can changing your mindset about this make you mentally stronger?

How would seeing rejection as applying to a concept (vs. yourself) make you mentally stronger *in real time* (that is, while it is happening)?

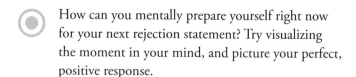

How can you mentally prepare yourself right now for your next rejection statement? Try visualizing the moment in your mind, and picture your perfect, positive response.

VICTORY LAP!

Part Three—Done! I want to encourage you to take the time to answer the questions in each chapter, and to really challenge yourself. Books don't make you better; application is what counts!

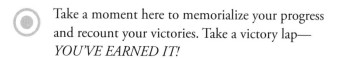

Take a moment here to memorialize your progress and recount your victories. Take a victory lap— *YOU'VE EARNED IT!*

DAILY JOURNAL NOTES

CLOSING 2.0

PART 4: CLOSING 2.0 PROCESS AND TECHNIQUE

DAY SEVENTEEN:

The Closing Progression

"Closing starts on the first call."
—Ken Thoreson, Acumen Management

A good friend of mine writes music for movies and television. You probably don't know the name, Brian Steckler, but you have likely heard his work.

In an interesting conversation, Brian has told me how composers develop individual musical themes for main characters. This is a very common approach and if you listen for it, you can easily hear the recurrence of specific themes throughout well-orchestrated movies.

This practice dates back hundreds of years, originating in opera. The goal of composers (like Brian) is to enhance the story and mood of a visual work of art with audio cues. Try turning off the sound during an especially emotional or tense part of any movie. It becomes immediately obvious how important a musical score is to the overall effectiveness of the visual story.

The same can be said for a good sales presentation. There are recurring themes throughout. One such theme could be labeled "agreements." The customer is drawn into a pattern of decisions, each building on the last. A cadence emerges.

I call this the *decision-making rhythm*. Without this steady rhythm, it's like someone has turned off the sound during your sales performance!

We've already discussed how closing is not a moment, but rather a process. The decision-making rhythm describes this process. It is the natural progression that can be found in any good sales presentation. As salespeople, we need to see that progression clearly before we can execute it.

> **The customer is drawn into a pattern of decisions, each building on the last.**

FINDING THE PROGRESSION

To begin, it is helpful to identify the most obvious milestones in your sales presentation.

If you were to diagram your typical sales path on a white board, where would the key moments be found *from your customer's perspective*? You can identify these moments by observing the customer's emotional altitude.

For example, if you are selling recreational vehicles you can sense your customer's emotional altitude in the early discovery: when he first sees an actual RV on the lot; when he steps inside the unit and is hit with an awesome first impression; when he finds cool features; when he sits in the driver's seat for the first time. Wouldn't it be cool if we could confirm agreement of value at each of those stages?

Of course, your closing questions won't be limited to those moments, but this outline gives you a good starting point. You can lay out the steps in a typical buying conversation and think about an agreement question for each one. (You'll find more help in formulating these questions in the chapters that follow.)

CLOSING IN PARTNERSHIP

Throughout this process, you'll want to keep in mind an important principle: Think of yourself as being side-by-side with your customers rather than face-to-face. You are simply guiding them on the journey, and you know you won't lead them into dangerous places.

The ultimate progression leads to a final close (Chapter 23). The final close will be so much easier if you've followed a natural progression to get there.

THE BIG IDEA:

Closing is a progression, not a moment in time.

APPLICATION EXERCISE:

 Take some time to lay out your sales presentation and identify the critical milestone moments. Then craft a closing question for each moment. Make sure the questions don't sound like you read them in a sales book somewhere. Make them relational and consistent with your own voice. Practice out loud; it will make a *huge* difference!

DAILY JOURNAL NOTES

. . . .

. . . .

. . . .

. . . .

. . . .

. . . .

. . . .

. . . .

. . . .

. . . .

. . . .

. . . .

. . . .

. . . .

. . . .

. . . .

. . . .

. . . .

. . . .

DAY EIGHTEEN:

Why Discovery Drives Closing

"The inability to close is a direct result of poor needs development. It is the symptom of the problem, not the actual problem itself."
—Jill Konrath, author of *Agile Selling*

True story: A new home sales representative asked the following question of an older couple: "Why are you thinking about moving?" The couple was stumped at first, unsure of how to answer. After a slightly awkward amount of time elapsed, the husband said, "You know, I've never bought a new home in my life, which means my wife has never had the opportunity to make a house her own."

The best part of that story came the next day when the husband came back to the office and told the salesperson, "No one has ever asked me why we are moving. And because I hadn't been asked, I had never clarified that for myself. Your question helped me to gain clarity as to why we are making this move in the first place."

What does this story have to do with closing? Plenty. Sometimes the customer's mission is clear; sometimes it is vague. His vision must become clear in order for a sale to occur.

Making minor closes during the discovery process produces a clear vision for your customer.

DISCOVERY AND CLOSING— THE CONNECTION

Most salespeople don't see the direct relationship between discovery and closing. The truth is, those who are best at closing are best at discovery. They gain agreements based on what they know about the customer, so the close is custom tailored to the situation.

Out of all you need to learn about your customers, there is nothing more important than a deep understanding of their motivation. Why are they looking to purchase in the first place?

What is happening in their lives that caused them to take action? Why are they talking to you?

Everything else is just details.

> *"Closing the deal is the natural next step if you've qualified well."*
> —Lynn Hidy, upyourtelesales.com

But note that there exists an opportunity during the discovery to strike a powerful closing chord.

> Out of all you need to learn about your customers, there is nothing more important than a deep understanding of their motivation.

ADVANCED TECHNIQUE

If you want to maximize the opportunity to gain agreements during the closing process, focus on these two techniques:

1. Ask a question that summarizes what is wrong.

It's one thing for your customers to explain their motivation (their mission). It's a far more powerful thing for you to summarize it back to them. Think of a question that starts with, "So if you stay where you are, you'll have to put up with…" Or, "So if you do nothing at this point, you'll continue to struggle with…" The magic lies in helping the customers to summarize their own pain, thus leading them to that point of inevitability where they determine that the pain *must* be resolved.

2. Ask a question that summarizes what needs to be right.

Immediately following the "what's wrong" question, summarize what the bright future could look like. "So I would need to show you something that offers…" Or, "If you're going to accomplish your goals, you need to find something that allows you to…" This question is not so much driven by products or features as it is by Future Promise, the promise of a better life.

These are simple and conversational questions. They are not heavy-handed or dramatic.

Your customers will appreciate that you understand their position, but the more important benefit is that the customers will agree *with themselves!*

THE BIG IDEA:

The earlier you begin to ask closing
questions, the clearer the vision
becomes for your customer.

APPLICATION QUESTIONS:

When do you ask your first closing question in a
typical sales presentation? How could you advance
that and ask a question sooner in the process?

How early in your sales process do you seek to
understand a customer's buying motivation—his
mission? Could you advance that and do it earlier in
the process?

Think of a common buying scenario, perhaps taken
from a recent customer. Write out an appropriate
question that summarizes what is wrong, and then
write a second question that summarizes what needs
to be right.

DAILY JOURNAL NOTES

. . . .

. . . .

. . . .

. . . .

. . . .

. . . .

. . . .

. . . .

. . . .

. . . .

. . . .

. . . .

. . . .

. . . .

. . . .

. . . .

. . . .

. . . .

. . . .

. . . .

DAY NINETEEN:

Minor Agreements with Major Payoffs

"Friendly negotiation with the intent to find the best solution for all parties usually results in acquiring the sale, along with a loyal clientele."
—Elinor Stutz, CEO of *Smooth Sale*, speaker and author

> Minor agreements during the
> sales process serve as progress
> indicators. They show me that I am
> on track, zeroing in on my target.

Is there anything more arduous than the drive home after a long trip? I have family in the San Francisco Bay area and I live between Sacramento and Lake Tahoe, three hours inland. I make the drive go faster by spotting specific landmarks along the way. I always look for these markers:

- The Benicia Bridge
- The Nut Tree in Vacaville
- Cal State University at Davis
- Downtown Sacramento

- Skatetown Ice Arena (where I play hockey!)

- Old Town Newcastle

- Home

Looking for these landmarks confirms my progress and verifies that I am getting closer to my goal.

See where I'm going here?

Minor agreements during the sales process serve as progress indicators. They show me that I am on track, zeroing in on my target.

THINK INEVITABILITY

The great part about minor agreements is that they make the final agreement virtually inevitable. After all, it would be illogical to agree with everything along the way but then disagree to the purchase decision (just as it wouldn't be logical *not* to go home after the long drive). If the progression holds its course, the final close is the obvious destination. This is where a progression mentality pays off.

> The great part about minor agreements is that they make the final agreement virtually inevitable.

PROGRESSION QUESTIONS— KEEP THEM SIMPLE

These questions don't need to be complicated. In fact, they are most effective when they are simple. The best minor agreements are natural and conversational. You may not expect to see sample questions like these in a sales technique book, but the point is, you should be thinking in terms of common vernacular:

- "Is that cool or what?"

- "Do you just love how this works?"

- "Isn't that awesome?"

- "Neat, huh?"

That's right. "Neat, huh?" is a perfectly acceptable closing question, so long as the customer's head nods north and south. Agreement gained!

Translate these questions into your own verbal style. Be sure to take the sales hat off for a spell and just enjoy the process with your customer. Have fun with this; make it an enjoyable agreement of value.

NEED – VALUE – AGREEMENT

As you progress in the process, you can expand on the minor closes by tying them into what you learned about the customer initially.

Think of minor closes in three parts: need, value, and agreement.

1) Need. "You had said you had a problem with…"

2) Value. "This feature allows you to…"

3) Minor Agreement. "Is that great, or what?"

Practice this technique by thinking of a value point you regularly share and then incorporate it into the customer's mission using need / value / agreement questions. It's powerful, it's effective, and it's fun!

Great salespeople are in the habit of
gaining agreements and, in so doing,
they make it easy for customers to buy.

THE DECISION-MAKING HABIT

Using minor closes establishes a decision-making rhythm. But it's more than just a rhythm; it's a decision-making *habit*. Great salespeople are in the habit of gaining agreements and, in so doing, they make it easy for customers to buy.

> ### THE BIG IDEA:
> **Minor agreements make the
> final agreement inevitable.**

APPLICATION QUESTIONS:

- Typically, how aware are you of the progression of closing questions in your own presentation? Where could you place more minor closes?

- Is it difficult to keep your language simple and smooth in your presentation? Consider practicing asking these questions out loud, in your normal, conversational tone and voice.

- Think of a recent customer interaction and replay it using the Need-Value-Agreement technique.

DAILY JOURNAL NOTES

DAY TWENTY:

Closing as Problem-Solving

"Change is not made without inconvenience, even from worse to better."
—Samuel Johnson

I had the great privilege of writing the sales presentation for The Villages of Florida, the largest active adult community in the world. One thing I can tell you about that buyer profile is that they are *not* in a hurry. These folks are facing a major decision at a crucial time of life and they don't want to make a mistake. Getting these tentative buyers unstuck was my challenge.

Here is one question that proved effective in this situation: "What happens if you do nothing?"

This question leads customers to face the realities of inevitability. If they stay where they are, their pain points do not get resolved. Clarifying that doing nothing is not a viable option frees customers up to move forward.

Every close must solve a problem in the customer's life.

YOUR CUSTOMER'S MISSION

*"The closeness of the decision attests
the measure of doubt."*
—Benjamin Nathan Cardozo,
U.S. Supreme Court Justice

Why is your customer talking to you? What happened to bring her into your office / store / sales center? I can tell you with complete certainty that her goal—her mission—is to improve her life. Your goal is to help your customers help themselves.

So here's the next big concept to get your head around: Every close must solve a problem in the customer's life. The close brings a conclusion to whatever was wrong.

Let's revisit the sales process for a recreational vehicle. Suppose you are selling RVs and you have a customer who is concerned about where to store the thing. First you find the best solution, then you ask the summary question to confirm that the issue is resolved: "Not only would you not have to keep it on your own property, but shared RV storage facilities are much more secure. *So does that solve the problem for you?*"

Suppose you sell vacation homes. You have a customer whose current aggravation is dealing with inconsistent hotels. You can build on a positive solution to this problem with a sentence like this: "What's great is that you mentally begin your vacation earlier because you know everything is just where you want it to be. *That would be a nice change, wouldn't it?*"

PROVIDING COGNITIVE EASE

With each problem you solve you move your customer from doubt to security, from stress to relief, from fearful to confident. As each dilemma is erased, you will find that your customer is in a much healthier frame of mind when it comes to making the final decision.

I suggest you identify some common problems your customers face and then come up with sample closes aimed at cementing the solutions. These are (probably) not final closes just yet. But they are getting you powerfully close to the target.

THE BIG IDEA:

Every close must solve a problem in the customer's life.

APPLICATION QUESTIONS:

Do you see yourself, at least in part, as a counselor? How does the counselor mindset make you more effective as a sales professional?

How much of your job involves solving customers' problems? How can you more effectively ask questions which confirm the solution?

Get together with a teammate (or several) and brainstorm situations where you are solving problems for your customers. Then think of the best solution questions to summarize.

DAILY JOURNAL NOTES

DAY TWENTY-ONE:

"Almost There" Agreements

Years ago I took my family on a weekend drive to Mount Diablo State Park, inland about 30 miles from San Francisco. We stopped to take advantage of an incredible view on a gorgeous spring day. I noticed a man painting a picture at the side of the road and engaged him in a conversation that soon became a sales pitch.

At one point I said, "It's a lot of money and I didn't come up here thinking I was going to spend anything at all." He replied, "I get it. But here's the thing. This painting is going to hang in a gallery and hundreds—perhaps thousands—of people will look at and, hopefully, admire it. And mark my words; someone will buy it. But I can promise you that this painting will never mean more to anyone on the planet than it does to you right here, right now."

That was a powerful statement! But was it a close? Let's think back to our definition from chapter 3:

Closing is the process of gaining agreements throughout the sales conversation, culminating in a final agreement to purchase.

Based on that definition, it was not a final close. There was not yet a final agreement, and if there was, it would have been up to me to present it.

What the artist offered me was what I call an "almost there" close. I use this close when I get that feeling in my gut that I am close to a final agreement, but I want to make sure any and all issues (objections) are out of the way.

> ## The trial close makes the final close, well, inevitable.

TRIAL CLOSE OR FINAL CLOSE?

Almost there closes (what others call test or trial closes) are commonly taught, and with good reason. The purpose of the almost there close is to make the final close inevitable. (There's that word again.)

Warning: Sometimes trial closes get used in place of final closes. Don't do this!

Example: "Is there anything standing in your way or holding you back?" This isn't a bad question, assuming you are asking with sincere interest, but is it a final close? Nope. It fails the test of our definition.

How about this question: "How are you feeling right now? Are you excited about the possibility of owning this?" That is a powerful almost there close, but it is not a final close.

On the other hand, how could you NOT ask a final close with each of the last two trial closes? The trial close makes the final close, well, inevitable.

THE "EXPLAIN THE PROCESS" CLOSE

Sometimes the last step in making a decision is simply understanding the purchase process.

While you sell every day, your buyer may purchase what you sell only on rare occasions. The Explain the Process close works just as it sounds. Simply walk the customer through the purchase process and end with an agreement on next action.

For example, suppose you are selling custom, upscale jewelry. Your close might sound something like this: "Should you decide to purchase, let me explain the steps. First, we pick out the specific setting… (Fill in the details of the process, but keep it brief)…and then we deliver your finished jewelry to your home. Does that all make sense to you?" In this case I have not asked for the sale, but I have set up the final close so I can easily transition into asking for the sale.

If the customer agrees, I then ask for the final agreement by going back to that first step in the process. "Great. So the very next step is to pick out the setting. Are you ready to begin?"

Be careful…but not too careful. When your gut says it's time to close, don't overthink it. But if you sense that an "almost there" close would be in your customer's best interest, go for it.

THE BIG IDEA:

Trial closes make the final close inevitable.

APPLICATION QUESTIONS:

Do you sometimes feel your anxiety level rising when you are nearing the final close question? How can an almost there close help build your confidence?

Take some time to list all the steps in the purchase process. Turn that list into an Explain The Process close. Practice it repeatedly.

What other almost there closes would work in your business?

DAILY JOURNAL NOTES

DAY TWENTY-TWO:

When to Ask for the Sale

*"If you're offered a seat on a rocket ship, you
don't ask what seat. You just get on."*
—Eric Schmidt, CEO of Google

WHEN TO CLOSE?

You are deep into a sales conversation with a prospect. She clearly likes what you have to offer. Because you were thorough in the discovery phase, you have a deep understanding of her motivation, her Current Dissatisfaction and her Future Promise. The price, timing, and terms are all good.

And BOOM! There it is—the voice in your head. As if by magic, a nearly audible voice says, "This is a good time to ask for the sale!"

We all know the voice. We've all heard it. The voice isn't faint or subtle. You just need to believe it. When the voice goes off, it is time to ask for the sale.

Think about it: Do you ever hear the voice at the beginning of the process? Of course not. Nor in the middle. The voice goes off when the customer is at a point of sky-high emotional altitude.

The voice goes off when the customer is feeling strong and positive about buying. The salesperson who is *truly* in tune with his customer will sense this and he will act without pause or hesitation.

When should you ask for the sale? Whenever the voice in your head makes even the slightest suggestion to do so.

WHERE TO CLOSE?

You're on a test drive. You savor the new car smell. You tune the radio to your favorite station. You look at your reflection in the mirror-like, perfect exterior. You can mentally picture the reactions of your coworkers when you pull up to work in your new ride. It's a wonderful emotional journey! Or at least it *should* be.

Making a purchase decision should be fun, don't you think? Especially for an emotional purchase. So why is it the practice in most industries to close the deal in the most uncomfortable place possible—the closing office?

It's ironic to me. Salespeople agree that customers buy on emotion and support their decision with logic. I hear that all the time. So why do we feel the need to remove the emotion from the close by having the final agreement take place in a sterile, uncomfortable, completely unemotional setting?

If you are looking for the perfect setting in which to ask for the sale, simply go back to the place where the emotional altitude was at its highest point. Stand in the kitchen. Sit in the car. Wrap the designer watch around his wrist. Hand her the stinkin' puppy, for cryin' out loud!

Customers enjoy the process most when their emotional altitude is at its highest point. So, go there!

YOU MUST EARN THE RIGHT...

We've all sat through a training class where we were taught, "You must earn the right to ask for the sale." Please, I beg you, get that thought out of your mind. It will only slow you down. The only thing this advice will do is make you second-guess whether the time is right.

By the time the voice goes off in your head, *you have already earned the right*. The voice wouldn't be speaking if you hadn't. How do we know this? Because you are not asking for you; *you are asking for your customer*. The voice is telling you to serve the person standing in front of you and to make it easy for that customer to purchase.

THE AUTO-RESPONSE

Think back to the last time you heard the voice. What did you do? How did you react? Did you have an automatic response in mind, or did the voice trip you up? Now think ahead to the next time you will hear the voice. How can you respond effectively?

Ask for the agreement at a time of high emotional altitude and everyone wins.

> ### THE BIG IDEA:
> **When you ask for the sale,
> you serve the customer.**

APPLICATION QUESTIONS:

In your sales practice, do you often find that the final agreement takes place in a setting of low emotion? If so, can you change the environment to raise the emotion level?

How do you respond when the voice goes off in your head? What would be an even better response?

Think about your typical sales conversation. When is the voice most likely to speak? How can you mentally prepare yourself for that moment?

DAILY JOURNAL NOTES

DAY TWENTY-THREE:

The Final Close

"Take time to deliberate, but when the time for action has arrived, stop thinking and go."
—Napoleon Bonaparte

Congrats, you've made it! Or perhaps you just skipped ahead to today. Whatever—you're here, so let's go.

So here it is, the big reveal… The Jeff-Shore-Super-Secret-Final-Knock'EmDead-ScoreboardBaby-Close! Here's what you do: Turn to the customers and give them a smug smile. Wink. Pause for 1.5 seconds, then reach down, hitch up your pants and say, "What's it gonna take to get you to buy my product today?"

Emphasize the word "you," and be sure to point at them with both hands (index fingers out, thumbs up, like a couple of guns). Then shut up, because as we have all been taught, the next person who speaks…

If you've been reading the book up to this point you know that this is the polar opposite of anything I would ever espouse!

In fact, I'm afraid you're in for a letdown. Because this isn't rocket science, and there isn't some silver bullet, one-size-fits-all question that will assure you of sales success.

The final close is relational. It is an extension of the relationship you have developed with your customer. It is the natural culmination of everything that has happened up to that point. But "natural" does not in any way mean you should "just let it happen."

> The mindset of a great salesperson
> is one of satisfaction in helping
> customers fulfill their mission.

THE SELF-TEST

Asking for the sale is more about intent than it is about technique. At the time of the final close are you feeling:

- Joyful?

- Satisfied?

- Confident?

- Serving?

- Proud?

If you are seriously stressed when the voice in your head is telling you to ask for the sale, you're doing it wrong. Asking for the sale must be a time of calm confidence and positive energy. The mindset of a great salesperson is one of satisfaction in helping customers fulfill their mission.

THE AUTO-RESPONSE

That said, there must be no pause or hesitation when the voice in your head tells you, "It's time." You need an auto-response, a go-to question that you are not making up on the fly. This question should be smooth, natural, simple, and most importantly, relational. And it has to confirm that the customer has agreed to purchase. Craft your go-to question and practice it out loud over and over.

The benefit in the auto-response, for you *and* for your customer, is confidence. You can ask for the sale without any stress on your part, stress that could be transferred to your buyer.

PREPARING FOR THE MOMENT

The final close requires mental preparation on your part. It might sound like a strange concept, but you can prepare for this moment by relying on the principles of Cognitive Behavioral Therapy. This popular therapeutic approach to brain training teaches that you can plan and rehearse your mental response in advance of a potentially stressful moment. In other words, you can decide *right now* how you will respond when the voice tells you to ask for the sale. You can decide how you will feel, what you will say, and how you will respond to the customer's answer.

If you decide these things now, before the stress of the closing moment sets in, you will make a choice from the logical side of your brain. If you are unprepared when the voice goes off, you will likely respond from the emotional side of your brain. That part of your brain desires comfort, and it will suggest (strongly) that you back off from asking for the sale.

(If this topic resonates with you, consider reading my sales psychology book, *Be Bold and Win the Sale*.)

DO IT!

Be aware of this: Very, VERY few sales are lost because sales-people are too assertive.

In those rare cases, the loss happens because the relational foundation is not strong. But you love your customers and they love you right back. Do them a favor—ask them to buy!

RESOURCES

My guess is that some of you might be feeling let down right now. You've come to the "Final Close" part of the book and there are no, well, final closes. Let me offer two suggestions.

First, think about how you would ask for the sale from your best friend. However you would do that with him or her, do the same with your customer.

Your relationship with your BFF is personal, of course, so the wording will be unique to you. It might sound something like, "You know I wouldn't steer you wrong; I think you should do this." Or perhaps, "I can't make the decision for you, but I think this is the right thing to do. What do you think?"

Or with *really* close relationships, "C'mon, ya knuckle-head—what are you waiting for?!" The point is to *be relational* when you close.

Second, if you are looking for specific wording examples you can consult any number of well-written books on the subject, including:

- Jeffrey Gitomer's *Very Little but Very Powerful Book on Closing*
- Brian Tracy's *The Art of Closing the Sale*
- Tom Hopkins' *Sales Closing for Dummies*

- Zig Ziglar's *Secrets of Closing the Sale*

The point here is this: you can memorize all the best closing lines in the world. But they won't amount to a hill of beans if you don't build your sales presentation for a confident closing moment from the very first handshake.

Get that part right and you'll be ready to change someone's world!

THE BIG IDEA:

The final close is a relational question, not a sales-y question.

APPLICATION QUESTIONS:

Have old-school methods left you feeling like "closing" is a dirty word? Do you ever have negative thoughts at the time of the close? What would change that?

How strong is your "auto-response" question? What can you do to cement that question in your brain so you don't pause or hesitate?

Take some time to visualize your sales process and put yourself in the closing moment. Plan for your mental response first, and then say the closing question out loud, feeling confident and joyful when you do.

DAILY JOURNAL NOTES

. . . .

. . . .

. . . .

. . . .

. . . .

. . . .

. . . .

. . . .

. . . .

. . . .

. . . .

. . . .

. . . .

. . . .

. . . .

. . . .

. . . .

. . . .

. . . .

DAY TWENTY-FOUR:

Second Chances

"Don't panic when a prospect exhibits last-minute hesitation. Just stay focused on what they value and how you deliver that value."
—Jeff Beals, author of *Selling Saturdays* and *Self Marketing Power*

Kid: "Can I have some candy?"
Dad: "No."
Kid: "Please?"
Dad: "No."
Kid: "I'll be good."
Dad: "No."
Kid: "Mommy would say yes."
Dad: "OK."

What is it about kids that causes them to simply disregard the word "no"? And at what point in our lives do we lose that drive?

Do you have a standard response when a customer says no? How can you improve it?

In Chapter 16 I addressed the subject of rejection, describing the important difference between rejecting a concept and rejecting a person. In sales, a rejection simply means that something is not yet resolved in the customer's mind.

A rejection also means there is more work that needs to be done. Asking for the sale is not the end of the process; solving the customer's problem is the end of the process.

THE CLOSING CYCLE™

When a customer says no, this should not signal any kind of finality. If the customer had already actively eliminated your offering, she would no longer be participating in the process. Get it out of your mind that there is an irrevocability to the word "no."

Instead, adopt a strategy for what to do when you get a "no." For years I have taught sales professionals to follow The Closing Cycle™ in these four steps:

1) Close – Ask for the sale when the voice tells you to do so.

2) Objection – Ask why the customer said "no." Keep it relational and comfortable.

3) Resolve – Solve the objection and confirm that the issue is resolved.

4) Close Again – Ask a second time, still naturally and relationally.

I call it The Closing Cycle™, but as a way to remember it, you might consider the acronym CORC (Close, Objection, Resolve, Close).

CORC-ING EXAMPLE

This is what The Closing Cycle™ might look like if you were selling new homes:

Sales Pro: *Would you like to move forward and purchase homesite 34?" (CLOSE)*

Prospect: *"I don't think we're ready to do that right now."*

Sales Pro: *"Fair enough, but I know you're very interested and I want to help. Tell me what's holding you back." (OBJECTION)*

Prospect: *"We're concerned about the timing. It will take six months to build this home and we were hoping to be in by the start of the school year."*

Sales Pro: *"Got it. And thanks for sharing that with me. You know, there are always trade-offs when you are purchasing a home; it's never a perfect scenario. You have to ask yourself whether you want to buy something that is already built—you don't get to make any design choices—or if you would rather have the home you really want. What is more important, the timing or the finished home?" (RESOLVE)*

Prospect: *"We really want to design it ourselves."*

Sales Pro: *"I thought so. Shall we put a sold sign on homesite 34 for you?"* (CLOSE)

Sales Pro: *"Yeah, let's do it!"* (HUG)

I want to point out that everything the salesperson did in this example was *in the customers' best interest.* No tricks, no manipulation. Just helping the customers to solve the problem in a way that best served their interests.

Of course, in many cases it might take some time to get an objection resolved; not everything comes together as cleanly as in the example. It doesn't mean it's not going to happen.

The key is to stay focused on the goal. Your objective is not to ask for the sale; that is simply part of the process. Your objective is to complete the customer's mission, regardless of how many closing attempts it takes.

If you are 100% committed to serving, it will be difficult for the customer to think about buying from someone else. The greatest compliment I received when I was selling new homes was when people told me there were homes they liked more than those I sold, but that they didn't want to buy from another salesperson; they wanted to buy from me. Sweetness!

> Your objective is not to ask for the
> sale; that is simply part of the process.
> Your objective is to complete the
> customer's mission, regardless of how
> many closing attempts it takes.

IN SUMMARY

Tip One: Be positive when the customer says "no" or "not yet." Come back with a positive response that shows you are not thrown off. Continue the relationship-based partnership.

Tip Two: Don't hesitate to figure out what's going on. Dig deep, be curious, be a problem-solver. Take them through the CORC process.

Tip Three: Believe in a second attempt (and a third, and a fourth…)

THE BIG IDEA:

Close – Understand the Objection – Resolve the Issue – Close Again

---

APPLICATION QUESTIONS:

Do you have a standard response for when a customer says no? How can you improve it?

How do you imagine yourself using the CORC model? Come up with some examples and talk them through out loud.

Practice the CORC method with a peer or with your manager. Merely thinking it through isn't enough to effectively improve your technique. You need to practice under all kinds of different scenarios.

DAILY JOURNAL NOTES

DAY TWENTY-FIVE:

The Celebration

Consider this scenario…

Tom: *"Maggie, will you marry me?"*

Maggie: *"Oh yes, Tommy. I would love to be your wife."*

Tom: *"Well, with that out of the way, let's discuss the process and logistics as to what happens next. We'll start with the legal issues, then move on to a discussion about the process of finding wedding vendors, and then we can dive into the financial discussions. Shall we?"*

What kind of cold-hearted… I mean, c'mon. I think we can all agree that at least a hug was in order before ol' Tom started down the logistics road!

With that silly example setting the stage, consider what happens all too often in the purchase process:

Customer: *"We'll take it."*

Salesperson: *"Okay. Let's get the paperwork started."*

Paperwork? Really? These good folks just made a major purchase decision, having gone through an emotional process, and you want to throw a stack of paperwork in front of them? How Tommy of you.

> An emotional decision in an emotional
> time suggests an emotional response.
> So why do so many salespeople treat
> the consummation of a sale with all the
> joy and celebration of a tax audit?

SHARING THE JOY

The reality is that while the customers might be feeling some angst about a major purchase decision, they are simultaneously feeling excited, maybe even *really* excited! They just agreed to the solution that will solve their problem. Their search is over. Their mission is complete.

Are you there to share the joy with them?

An emotional decision in an emotional time suggests an emotional response. So why do so many salespeople treat the consummation of a sale with all the joy and celebration of a tax audit? Purchase decisions are giant opportunities to insert the joy that is all too often missing.

CEMENTING THE MOMENT

There are countless ways to memorialize big purchase moments. What can you do to celebrate before you get into the procedural part of the purchase process?

Consider the car seller who carries a large "SOLD" placard and allows the customer to place it on the windshield. Or the furniture salesperson who snaps a picture of the customers sitting on a brand new sofa (even though they've just ordered a custom covering that will take eight weeks). Or the golf club sales professional who gives his customers who buy a new set of clubs a gift certificate for a round of golf at a local upscale course.

Memorializing a moment doesn't have to cost anything, it just has to, ya know, be joyful! Sometimes it is as simple as a very reaffirming, reassuring statement like, "I am so happy for you two. You are going to absolutely love this." (Cue Kleenex.)

> The best way to provide meaningful moments of joy for your customers is to think in terms of experiences rather than processes.

THINK "EXPERIENCE"

The best way to provide meaningful moments of joy for your customers is to think in terms of experiences rather than processes. Your customers (and you) value experiences above all else and great experiences make for great stories. What stories do you want your customers to tell about their purchase experience? What can you do at the point of sale that would be, literally, remark-able.

Your task is to burn the purchase moment into your customer's brain in a positive, joy-filled way.

> What stories do you want your customers to tell about their purchase experience?

THE BIG IDEA:

An emotional decision deserves an emotional response.

APPLICATION QUESTIONS:

How strategic is your process for responding to a "yes?" Are you satisfied with the way you handle that now?

Is your response at the close typically emotional or procedural? Do you allow yourself to be caught up in the moment along with your customers? What can you do to be more emotionally engaged?

Spend some time today brainstorming ways to cement the decision and memorialize the moment. Talk to your peers or to your manager. Make it special!

DAILY JOURNAL NOTES

DAY TWENTY-SIX:

Keeping the Sale Closed

"Abnormal behavior in abnormal situations is normal."
—Viktor Frankl

We all have second thoughts.
It's a normal part of life. So why
do we struggle so much when
our customers do the same?

The scene: a hotel room in Hawaii at 1:35 a.m. A husband sits up suddenly. "Oh, dear Lord. What did we do? A fractional vacation ownership? Really? We bought a time-share? We said we would never do such a thing. And we did. It seemed like such a good idea at the time. Is it still? Should we go through with this????"

Second thoughts. It's a phrase we are all familiar with.

"On second thought, I think I'll have the chicken."

*"I wanted to marry her, and I never
gave it a second thought."*

"I was going to vacation in the Bahamas but, on second thought, decided on the Virgin Islands."

We all have second thoughts. It's a normal part of life. So why do we struggle so much when our customers do the same?

REMORSE HAPPENS

From a psychological perspective, remorse sets in when the buying formula gets out of whack. Remember that customers follow a subconscious mental model when making purchase decisions: Current Dissatisfaction x Future Promise > Cost + Fear.

At the time of the decision the formula is weighted to the left side of the equation. But sometimes, things tilt back to the right *after* the decision has been made. We know of this as buyer's remorse.

PREVENTING BUYER'S REMORSE

What can we do to prevent buyer's remorse from happening? Here are three ideas:

1) *Memorialize the moment.* We talked about this in the last chapter's lesson in our discussion on sharing the joy with your customer. An additional benefit is that taking the time to celebrate and make a memory inspires an emotional investment for buyers that serves to keep the sale sold. Simply put, memorializing something makes it seem more real, which helps stave off buyer's remorse.

2) *Get the customer to make a public commitment.* I'm seeing this more and more on my Facebook feed. A couple standing next to their brand new car, with the dealership sign strategically placed in the background. People announce to the whole world (Facebook IS the world, right?) that they have made this decision. Such announcements make it more difficult to go back on that choice. Another way to encourage commitment is to ask, "Is there someone you want to call to let them know you've made this important decision?"

3) *Warn the buyer of the reality of remorse.* Be the counselor and let the customers know of the side effects of a purchase decision. Tell them that buyer's remorse is both real and normal. But then tell them what to do about it. Encourage them to remember the feeling they had when they said "yes." If you did your job right, this will draw your customer back to a happy place and a better frame of mind.

Of course, there are times when a customer has a legitimate change of heart. The decision didn't feel right, and he becomes more and more uncomfortable as time passes. It happens. The question is whether you did your best to prevent that occurrence.

THE BIG IDEA:

**Emotions make the sale...
emotions keep the sale.**

APPLICATION QUESTIONS:

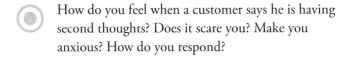

How do you feel when a customer says he is having second thoughts? Does it scare you? Make you anxious? How do you respond?

Which of the three ideas for preventing buyer's remorse could be most helpful for you?

Practice the buyer's remorse conversation with a peer or your manager. Don't wait until you have a customer trying to back out of an agreement before you attempt to come up with a response. Continual practice builds your confidence for crucial sales moments.

VICTORY LAP!

Part Four – Accomplished! We just uncovered a slew of technique opportunities. Hopefully you've already begun to make changes in your closing approach. Yes, there are always stumbles when we are trying something new, but that is not what we will focus on here.

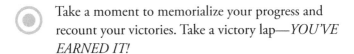

Take a moment to memorialize your progress and recount your victories. Take a victory lap—*YOU'VE EARNED IT!*

DAILY JOURNAL NOTES

CLOSING 2.0

PART 5: CLOSING 2.0 IN ACTION!

DAY TWENTY-SEVEN:

The Mastery Accelerator™

"To improve is to change. To be perfect is to change often."
—Winston Churchill

The one word you need to understand about the necessity of practice: Myelin.

Myelin is a mixture of proteins and phospholipids that forms an insulating sheath around nerve fibers, increasing the speed at which impulses are conducted. As an action is repeated over and over again, more myelin is created in the brain, causing impulses to move faster and more accurately. (For more on this fascinating topic, read Daniel Coyle's book, *The Talent Code*.)

The increase of myelin is the neurological basis of talent development. If you have ever taken music lessons, you know what I'm talking about. Those first repetitions of scales were clunky and uncomfortable. Over time, they became second nature. Why? Myelin in the brain.

I play ice hockey (or, as it is known in Canada, "hockey") but I started later in life. When I turned 52, I didn't even know how to skate. At the time of this writing I just turned 54 and I lead my league in assists. (Yes, it's a low-level beer league, but still!)

My success in hockey is based on one thing: myelin. I cannot count the number of mornings I have been out on the ice at 5:15 a.m., often alone, practicing the same techniques over and over again. Repeated crossovers—myelin. Shooting against the wall—myelin. Transitioning from forward to backward over and over—myelin.

YOUR MYELIN

It is no different in sales. In fact, you've subconsciously developed loads of myelin already. Think about the part of your sales presentation you have down solid. Maybe it's an objection that you are masterful at overcoming or a feature you keenly enjoy demonstrating. That's your myelin doing its thing.

This is the neuroscientific evidence for how to get better at sales. There is no shortcut. If mastery is the goal, repetition is the means. The destination called mastery is found on the road called repetition. And there is just no other way to get there. No shortcuts.

THE MASTERY ACCELERATOR™

> *"Practice yourself in little things; and thence proceed to greater."*
> —Epictetus

This is precisely why I created the Mastery Accelerator™ several years ago. It is a means of not only repeating an action, but doing so in increasingly difficult environments in order to grow stronger in your technique. Think of how weightlifters train: They progress by adding weight, and thus, increasing discomfort. You simply do not get better without stretching the bounds of your comfort zone!

Put another way, if it doesn't challenge you, it doesn't change you. There is no growth without discomfort.

The Mastery Accelerator™ is designed to be applied to one specific skill set at a time. Suppose you want to work on your "Explain the Process" close (chapter 21). You would start by writing it out in your own words, and then practice it in the following four stages.

Stage One: Practice *out loud* ten times, all alone. The goal is not to merely get through 10 repetitions; the goal is to get better each time. The first couple of times will be uncomfortable. Then you will begin to get into a rhythm. Establishing a rhythm means you are internalizing, and that means you are building up myelin. Go you!

Stage Two: Practice out loud with a colleague. I know this sounds uncomfortable, but you will have already practiced at least ten times on your own, so you will have already made significant improvement. Practice with a colleague, out loud, five times. Receive feedback each time and continue to hone your newfound skill.

Stage Three: Practice three times with your manager. This is more uncomfortable still, but with the feedback you received from your colleague you will be in good shape to practice with your manager. Remember, every repetition builds more myelin.

Stage Four: Demonstrate your new skill to your entire sales team. And don't worry—if your presentation to your sales manager was horrible, he or she would do you a favor and send you back to the drawing board before you embarrass yourself. But by now, you've got this down!

Here's the great news: How much easier will it be to implement this new skill when it really counts—when you are with a customer? Your confidence will be high, your enjoyment will be strong, and you will be far more effective in advancing the sale.

THE MASTERY ACCELERATOR™

Practice This EXACT Skill...	Repeat This Many Times...	Keep Count
	10x **Practice** a very limited and specific skill (overcoming a single objection, or explaining just one feature, for example) out loud and **into a voice recorder** ten consecutive times. Listen after each recording and make notes.	10. ☐ 5. ☐ 9. ☐ 4. ☐ 8. ☐ 3. ☐ 7. ☐ 2. ☐ 6. ☐ 1. ☐
	5x **Practice the same technique with a peer**, five times. Find someone who will be brutally honest with you and who will coach you for performance improvement.	5. ☐ 4. ☐ 3. ☐ 2. ☐ 1. ☐
	3x Ratchet up the discomfort: **practice three times with your sales manager.** Now you're into the fine-tuning, so pay close attention. You are honing in on perfection!	3. ☐ 2. ☐ 1. ☐
	1x **Demonstrate your perfected skill in front of the entire sales team.** You can do this...you've put in the necessary repetition. You've moved from the panic zone to the learning zone to the comfort zone.	1. ☐

If you are balking at the use of the Mastery Accelerator™, it's probably the comfort addict in you coming out. And look, if you have a better strategy for building myelin, please let me know!

Get out of your comfort zone. Make practice a priority!

> The destination called mastery is found on the road called repetition.

APPLICATION QUESTIONS:

What makes practice difficult for you? Discomfort? Boredom? Not knowing what to do? How can you remedy that?

Think of a sales skill you have mastered. How did you get to that level of performance? What is the next skill you could master?

Try using the Mastery Accelerator™ on a new skill, starting today. Start small. Pick a simple objective. Then try another. Consider making the Mastery Accelerator™ a staple of your toolbox.

DAILY JOURNAL NOTES

DAY TWENTY-EIGHT:

Practice Tips

*"Though a man be wise, it is no shame
for him to live and learn."*
—Sophocles

I mentioned that I recently started playing hockey. Come to find out, there is no end to the number of hockey practice drill ideas available online. One drill involves a 5-gallon bucket turned upside down. You simply bend down, place one hand on the bucket, skate, and then turn sharply around the bucket. The bucket stabilizes you while you learn how to make a sharp turn without "losing your edge." As you progress, you push the bucket farther and farther away from yourself, causing you to get farther out on the edges of the skate blade.

The point of that drill is to fall. Put another way, the point of that drill is to fail. It is the only possible way to test your limits. If you don't push the bucket far enough away, you will never fall. But then you will never improve, and you will never know what you are capable of.

PRACTICE IS FAILING

> *"Experience is the name everyone*
> *gives to his mistakes."*
> —Oscar Wilde

We live in a society that utters testosterone-laced edicts like "Failure is not an option." That's fine if you're trying to bring a rocket back to earth from a failed mission, but when it comes to skill development, failure is the *only* option. You will never improve if you never fail.

In fact, the progression of development requires failure! You can see why in the following four steps:

1) Failure

2) Frustration

3) Find

4) Fix

Where do you think most people struggle in that progression? In my strong opinion, they struggle at point #1. They rarely go out of their way to try new techniques, so they never fail, so they are never frustrated, so they have nothing to find, and therefore, nothing to fix. Alas, they are absolutely maxed out on their skill set. They will never improve.

THE SILICON VALLEY MANTRA

Consider a phrase that is often used by tech entrepreneurs in the Silicon Valley. It comes in different forms, but it generally goes like this: "Fail often, fail fast, fail forward." The theory is that you cannot innovate if you are not willing to fail.

The same principle holds true in skill development. My #1 practice tip for you is this: fail.

Following are some specific tips and ideas on how to practice the techniques in this book.

Please be prepared to fail! If you try something once and give up, or worse, if you try something once and say, "nailed it," you are maxed out on your proficiency. You might be good, but great is out of the question.

PRACTICE IDEAS

1) Real-Time Review

The moment you conclude a sales presentation, do a real-time review. Ask yourself, "Where was I uncomfortable? Where did I struggle?" Then reenact and practice that moment *right away.* Practice it out loud and consider using the Mastery Accelerator™ method. The sooner you evaluate and correct the behavior, the greater the impact. Make this immediate reviewing a habit.

2) Leverage Your Smart Phone

When you speak, you hear your voice internally. When you record yourself and play it back, you hear it externally. Hearing yourself externally allows you to pick up nuances, verbal tics, etc. that you should change. (And believe me, you will *want* to make changes once you hear yourself...we are our own worst critics!) This is a way to self-train and get on the path to constant performance improvement.

3) The Fist Pump

This is a mental trick that will teach your brain to embrace the failure that is so necessary to performance improvement.

When you are practicing some new technique and you screw up (and you *will* screw up), stop what you are doing, make a fist, and pull it down with a hearty "Yes!" A fist pump is a small reward, a reminder that you are willing to fail in order to succeed.

4) Record Victory Laps

I'm a huge believer in journaling; I've been doing it for 20 years. The best part about it is recounting my progress over time. The ironic part is that my victories often started out as failure and frustration. Journaling serves as a reminder that what feels like failure in the present is a victory waiting to happen.

5) Find Someone to Eavesdrop

Imagine a musician who never has an instructor listen to his performance. Or an athlete who never has a coach observing her skills. Outside influence is critical to your success. Other people will see things you do not. Here's the stretch goal: Ask someone to eavesdrop on one of your actual sales conversations, either live or on the phone. I guarantee she will have great input for you.

> *"Practice does not make perfect.*
> *Perfect practice makes perfect."*
> —Vince Lombardi Jr.

THE BIG IDEA:

Fail often. Fail fast. Fail forward.

APPLICATION QUESTIONS:

Do you practice because you are forced to do so by your manager? How often do you practice on your own initiative?

How does your perspective on practicing change if you think of failure as a good and necessary thing?

Pick one technique you can start working on today. Set your ego aside, embrace the discomfort, and give it all you've got!

DAILY JOURNAL NOTES

DAY TWENTY-NINE:

Accountability

"Knowledge and timber shouldn't be used till they are seasoned."
—Oliver Wendell Holmes

This past year I utilized four different coaches and mentor groups. I had a business coach to help with my entrepreneurial endeavors, a speaking coach to improve my platform speaking skills, a mastermind group of peers who have similar business models, and I joined a tribe of sales experts.

Why four? Because this meant four times the accountability. I had four times the number of people who would challenge me. Four times the resources for peer reviewing, bouncing ideas off of each other, etc. (Perhaps I should have had five!)

There is something powerful—almost mystical—about accountability. There is a level of performance you achieve when you are accountable to others that is otherwise extremely difficult (impossible?) to attain. Here's why.

HOW THE BRAIN WORKS

Your brain is an incredible energy-saving machine. Its #1 job is to keep you alive. One way it does this is to constantly look for the simplest means to accomplish any given task. In his book,

Thinking Fast and Slow, Daniel Kahneman calls this the "Law of Least Effort."

While your brain is willing to settle for "good enough," accountability partners aren't (at least the good ones). Accountability partners can push you harder because *it's not their brains that are in the way.*

MUSIC LESSONS

In my home office I have a piano and a bass guitar. I took piano lessons for a couple of years. Other than watching a few YouTube videos, I've never taken a bass guitar lesson in my life. What do you think I'm better at? Piano, of course. (Not great, mind you, but strong enough to play at church on Sundays, and that's a win for me!) I pick up the bass guitar and mess around with it from time to time, but I'm not getting any better.

The difference in my proficiency is all about accountability. Having someone there who will push me, encourage me, and see more in me than I see in myself makes the difference between just fiddling around and actually becoming proficient.

Thanks to the Internet, you can teach yourself just about anything these days. Nonetheless, the world is not filling up with virtuosos of all kinds. Why not? Because there is very little accountability when you are teaching yourself.

An accountability partner doesn't have to be paid but you will put more into it, and therefore get more out of it, if you are making an investment. In fact, this year I am significantly increasing my investment in coaching for my own professional development.

MY 75-10-10-5 PLAN

Several months ago, I wrote a highly shared blog post in which I describe my own method of financial budgeting. It looks like this:

- 75% of my income goes to living expenses, taxes, discretionary funds, etc.

- 10% is given to church, charity, etc.

- 10% goes to savings and investments

- 5% is invested in my own development

I encourage you to consider adjusting your budget to include a 5% investment in your own improvement. It will be, I assure you, the most rewarding investment you can make.

TAKE A BOLD STEP

Here is a bold idea you can implement right away, and at no cost. Start a mastermind group.

Find a small group of likeminded people who are dedicated to performance improvement and self-development. The number one requirement is that each is passionate. Then, follow these guidelines:

- Set a specific time to meet each and every week. For example, Monday morning from 7:00 a.m. to 8:00 a.m. Tell invitees that if they cannot commit to weekly attendance, they should decline the invitation. You can meet in person at a coffee shop, by phone, or by Google Hangout. (In person is most effective.)

- Start by asking for commitments for a set number of weeks. Eight is a good starting point. You can continue the group after that, but you'll want to continue only with people who are truly committed.

- Determine eight narrowly defined topics. You don't want to allow for tangents, so make sure you are clear on each week's discussion point.

- Tell all participants to check their egos at the door. This is not a boast-fest. Vulnerability is a key aspect to the effectiveness of a small group.

- Manage the conversation tightly. Don't let anyone dominate.

Forming a mastermind group could be one of the most powerful action steps you can take this year. I've been a part of several, and I have never been disappointed.

THE BIG IDEA:

"Accountability brings about response-ability."
—Stephen Covey

APPLICATION QUESTIONS:

Do you have someone in your life who holds you accountable? To what level? Is this someone who can strongly and deeply challenge you to be the best you can be?

Should you consider paying for a coach or program that will help you grow and stretch?

Talk with just one peer about starting a mastermind group and see how that goes. Then do the same with one more person.

DAILY JOURNAL NOTES

DAY THIRTY:

Where to Grow from Here

"The journey of a thousand miles begins with a single step."
—Lao-tzu

As you may recall from the beginning of this book, I said this is not so much a book as it is a journey. Here's the (very) good news: The journey isn't over. In fact, it is just getting started.

Sales veterans who have been in the business for decades say that when it comes to skill development, closing the sale is always a priority. Refining your closing technique is something you should focus on every single day that you work in sales.

Additionally, future buyers will be even more knowledgeable, more savvy, and more skeptical. This all adds up to the fact that closing techniques will continue to evolve, giving you a constant opportunity to grow and improve.

If you are waiting for a manager or a sales trainer to motivate you to ask for the sale, you will always fall short of your potential. You alone must take control of your own growth and advancement.

When you look back five or ten years from now, what do you want to say about your skill set? About your commitment to growth? About how easy you made it for your customers to purchase?

The answers to the questions about tomorrow depend on your dedication today.

YOUR CONFIDENCE METER

Look back to Chapter 5 where I gave you three assignments, the last of which was to rate your confidence. Specifically, it looked like this:

3) Last, and most importantly, I want you to rate your closing confidence. Which statement describes you best?

   a) Closing scares me, I'm not good at it, and I am not at all confident.

   b) My closing approach is okay, but I don't enjoy it and I feel awkward when I try.

   c) I can close when I need to, but it is not really natural for me.

   d) I close better than average, but I know I can still improve.

   e) Closing is my strongest attribute; I believe I have maximized my potential.

Where did you rate yourself when you first considered this question? If you have truly focused on applying both the mindset and techniques in this book, you should be seeing a boost in your closing confidence. That confidence makes you comfortable at the exact moment when your customer needs you to be poised and calm.

So there you have it—a new look at closing, 2.0-style. Might I suggest two things to you overachievers out there?

1) Go back and start over. You'll find new ideas and new applications on the second read.

2) Start a book club / study group. Find some like-minded peers who desire to improve their own performance and go on this 30-day journey with them, meeting once a week to discuss the results and encouraging each other every day. Imagine the impact!

And be sure to follow me online so that you're getting the latest and greatest strategies, techniques and tools to help you close more sales faster.

JeffShoreCommunity

@jeffshore

JeffShore

THE BIG IDEA:

Where will you grow from here?

ASSIGNMENT:

 Go out there and change someone's world today!

DAILY JOURNAL NOTES

RECOMMENDED READING:

"Woe be to him who reads but one book."
—George Herbert

SALES AND PSYCHOLOGY BOOKS

- *Why We Buy* by Paco Underhill. This book on "retail anthropology" studies the way people shop and make buying decisions. Very enlightening.

- *The Tipping Point* by Malcolm Gladwell. Incredible illustrations about how ideas turn into revolutions.

- *Influence: The Psychology of Persuasion* by Robert Cialdini. Fascinating studies from the world's foremost expert on influence theory. Great case studies, highly applicable to the sales arena.

- *The Inner Game of Selling* by Ron Willingham. Powerful book on the mental side of the sales business. You won't see yourself the same way again.

- *Thinking, Fast and Slow* by Daniel Kahneman. A deep and powerful insight into the workings of the brain by the Nobel Prize-winning founder of behavioral economics.

- *Activate Your Brain* by Scott Halford. A very readable understanding on how to tap into more of your gray matter.

SUCCESS AND MOTIVATION BOOKS

- *The 7 Habits of Highly Effective People* by Stephen Covey. By far the best book around on personal productivity. This is an "active read." Have a highlighter and notepad ready. If you want to improve your listening skills the book is worth buying just to read habit four: "Seek first to understand, then to be understood."

- *The Power of Full Engagement* by Jim Loehr and Tony Schwartz. These coaches of "corporate athletes" teach powerful principles on becoming more productive by engaging more fully... and then *dis*engaging more fully. A deep discussion on how to manage your energy levels.

- *The Compound Effect* by Darren Hardy. All about the little things in life that make a huge difference over time. One of the most inspiring books I've read in a long, long time.

- *Eat That Frog!* by Brian Tracy. Short but excellent book on overcoming procrastination and getting things done.